To all travellers:
May they realize that to keep the way open
for them is never as easy as it seems.

The author acknowledges, with thanks, the expert assistance and direction received from editor Audrey McClellan and all at Heritage House.

Carving the Western Path

Routes to Remember

R.G. Harvey

VICTORIA • VANCOUVER • CALGARY

Heritage House Publishing Company Ltd.
#108 – 17665 66A Avenue
Surrey, BC V3S 2A7
www.heritagehouse.ca

Library and Archives Canada Cataloguing in Publication

Harvey, R. G. (Robert Gourlay), 1922-
    Carving the western path: routes to remember/R.G. Harvey.
Includes bibliographical references and index.

ISBN-13: 978-1-894974-17-2
ISBN-10: 1-894974-17-4

    1. Transportation—British Columbia—History. I. Title.

HE215.Z7B712 2006   388.09711   C2006-904155-5

Edited by Audrey McClellan and Karla Decker
Book design and layout by Darlene Nickull
Cover design by Frances Hunter
Cover photo courtesy of the B.C. Ministry of Transportation

Printed in Canada

Heritage House acknowledges the financial support for its publishing program from the Government of Canada's Book Publishing Industry Development Program, Canada Council for the Arts, and the province of British Columbia through the British Columbia Arts Council and the Book Publishing Tax Credit.

BRITISH
COLUMBIA
ARTS COUNCIL
We acknowledge the support of the Province of British Columbia through the British Columbia Arts Council

The Canada Council | Le Conseil des Arts
for the Arts | du Canada

CONTENTS

List Of Maps And Drawings

INTRODUCTION

*I*n the latter decades of the 19th century, the settlement of the southern Interior of British Columbia was delayed by continent-wide economic downturns, as well as by its inaccessibility. This delay occurred in spite of evidence that good land for agriculture was to be had on the plateaus and in the valleys, and in spite of the hints and eventual discovery of mineral riches in the southeast corner of the province. Transportation was the key, and the six chapters that follow give accounts of the methods of getting to the Interior, their development and dangers, and the story of one group of very determined settlers. In all of these, the difference the passage of time makes is amazing.

In the first of these tales, The Road Down the Valley, we learn that only indistinct trails and no roads at all existed in the Okanagan Valley in 1858, when a band of 160 gold-seeking prospectors, mostly Americans, moved into the valley from the south. They were all well armed, and they regarded any Native people they met as enemies. At Okanagan Lake they ambushed a party of unarmed Natives as they came ashore and killed 10 or 12 of them.

Just 100 years later, near that same place, workers were completing a magnificent floating bridge across the lake in order to serve a populous community. The tale of the time in between relates the creation of the road down that valley, and it speaks of the lake and its wonderful lake steamers, and of the growth and history of that community.

In the next journey along a waterway, The Road Up the Lake, we learn of the development of a simple two-lane highway, never more than that, alongside Kootenay Lake. This road and lakeshore are only 130 miles east of the first, but they are as different as chalk is from cheese. This story is even more interwoven with the lake steamers, and it too is a wonderful part of the province and of its history.

In the third of our tales of transportation, The Crows Nest Railway, a railway is built in record time in 1898 in order to retain B.C.'s below-ground riches in Canada, rather than have them disappear south. The speed of this construction—a mile a day for a total of 194 miles—is all the more remarkable as the terrain was far from easy. The Crows Nest Railway shows that men with handpower and horsepower alone can still move mountains, or at least build their way through them.

Regarding Weather and Roads in B.C., it was 1859, just one year after the Americans came to the Okanagan, that the Royal Engineers turned away from building the first road in B.C. up the Coquihalla River and Boston Bar Creek valleys because of "the signs of fearsome snow falls"—in other words, avalanche paths—in which snow had wiped out trees as it thundered down the hillside. It took some 127 years, until 1986, before this threat was dealt with. This was achieved by the construction of a snow shed and huge diversion trenches and containment basins, all part of the Coquihalla Highway, and by using explosives to reduce snow on the slopes above the highway before it was a danger. In this tale of weather and roads we examine avalanches, ice jams, debris torrents, snow and ice removal, and glaciers and their effects on roads.

The challenge of transporting people and vehicles over water is described in The Other B.C. Ferries. This chapter records the history of the ferries run by the Department of Public Works (later the Ministry of Highways or Transportation), from ferries powered across rivers by human power or the force of the current, carrying no more than three or four cars, to those on Interior lakes propelled by engines of over a thousand horsepower and those of even greater power on coastal waters carrying 10 or 20 times as many vehicles.

Finally, The Trek of the Huscrofts in 1891 is the story of how one pioneer family moved to British Columbia in the early days, overcoming the trials of cross-country travel without roads, railways or ferries. They did it by horse and wagon, and on their river trip they used a raft.

These quick looks at B.C.'s fascinating transportation history tell of technical things and also of human resolution and determination in meeting nature's challenge.

CHAPTER 1

THE ROAD DOWN THE VALLEY

Rangelands, then fruit lands in a valley that was a nice, friendly place to live, held together by its highway.

*T*he Okanagan Valley has always had a special place in the hearts of British Columbians. There is no place quite like it in the province. Very few areas in B.C. have a climate quite so benevolent (most of the time), and nowhere are the lakes so blue—and not only blue, as Kalamalka Lake's wonderful greens show—or the combination of mountains and lakeshores so pleasant.

How did this valley develop into such a great place to live, and, related to that question, how were the roads to and down the valley built? First, it must be said that access was not all overland by any means. There was also access over water, with memorable results, particularly in the case of one unforgettable lake steamer; but this did not happen immediately.

The Aboriginals were, of course, the first people there, and from times past their trails were worn into the forests and grasslands. They had found pleasure, and good fishing, in their canoes on the multitude of lakes, which were both part of the river, like jewels on a necklace, and tributary to it.

The first White man on record in the valley was David Stuart, an American fur trader from Astoria, who accompanied David Thompson, the renowned British fur trader, explorer and map-maker. In 1811 the

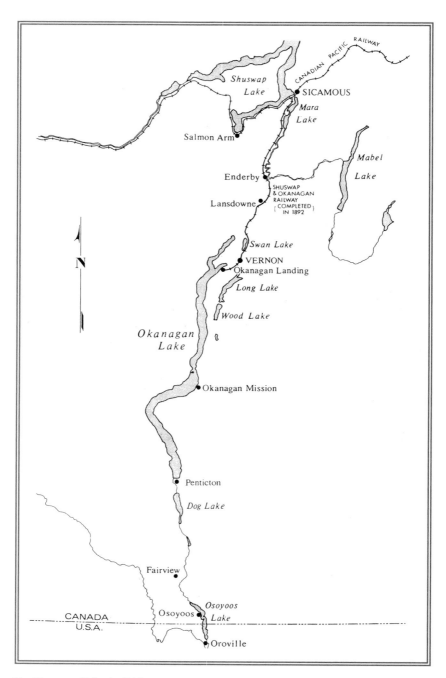

The Okanagan Valley in 1890

A view of Okanagan Lake

two of them were travelling back up the Columbia from its mouth. Thompson had just claimed the uplands of the huge river for the British Crown while on his way downstream to the coast.

Stuart left Thompson after they arrived at the Columbia's confluence with a lesser stream, known by a Native name that was spelled "Okanogan" south of the border and "Okanagan" in Canada. At the river junction, Thompson founded Fort Okanogan for the North West Company. He continued up the Columbia, and Stuart set off northward to explore this newfound waterway.

Crossing over what would become the international boundary 35 years later, Stuart came right up the lovely wide valley and, in due course, arrived at the place that became Fort Kamloops. Here he realized that he had discovered a wonderful route between the Pacific Ocean and the beaver-trapping area farther north, where several fur-trading posts had been established by the North West Company's Simon Fraser in what was then called New Caledonia.

The North West Company was absorbed by the Hudson's Bay Company 10 years later, but one year before that happened, in 1820, fur brigades started regular trips down the Okanagan Valley. Their route beside the southern half of the lake was along the top of the western hillside. The men of the brigades loved that part of the trip, "treading high above the shining waters" as they described it. They would see many shining waters from these heights, not just those of Okanagan Lake. From north to south they saw Swan Lake, Long Lake (later named Kalamalka) and Wood Lake. Then, beyond the south end of Okanagan Lake, they saw Dog Lake (now Skaha), Vaseux Lake and finally Osoyoos Lake.

The Fur Brigade Trail Down the Valley: (Present-day place names used.) The trail from Kamloops and Monte Creek ran down the west side of Okanagan Lake, close to the water's edge, as far as Peachland. It swung west at Deep Creek, going by Three Lakes and Garnet Valley, passing along the lower slopes of Mount Aeneas and Wild Horse Mountain, crossing over Trout Creek and then rising up over a height of land into the Shingle Creek and Marron valleys, which are located about four miles west of Kaleden Junction. The trail passed by White Lake and Meyers Flat and then along the east side of Osoyoos Lake to the present international border, which in those days took them into Washington Territory.

A quarter century later, in 1846, the international boundary was established and marked by the Royal Engineers. It ran through the middle of Osoyoos Lake, and this brought custom duties for the fur brigades that travelled along Okanagan Lake on their way to the mouth of the Columbia River. The HBC men at their headquarters in the east could not stand that for long, and they sought another route north of that border. Fort Langley came into being on the lower Fraser River, a different trail was established to that new overseas connection, and the lovely slopes along the blue waters of the Okanagan fell silent, but not for long.

In 1858 British Columbia was invaded by a force of outsiders who came up the Okanogan Valley from the south seeking gold. The word "force" is used because it was by no means peaceful. The members were mostly prospectors from northern

The Routes of the Fur Brigades: This map of northwest North America as it was from 1811 to 1861 shows the fur-trading routes of the time.

California, numbering close to 200, and they were even divided into companies, A, B, C, etc. They were all well armed.

The military nature of their travel through the western United States to get to B.C. was understandable, because that part of the nation was in a virtual state of war with the Native population then, mainly with the plains nations, but also with some of the adjoining tribes.

The force split up as soon as it crossed the 49th parallel. Some struck out westward, heading for the lower Fraser Valley, and the larger part, estimated at 160 in number, pressed on northward up the Okanagan

River valley. When either party met local Natives, they regarded them as the enemy and opened fire immediately.

G.P.V. and Helen Akrigg, in their *British Columbia Chronicle, 1847–1871*, describe an ambush set by this party on the banks of Okanagan Lake when they observed some Natives coming ashore in canoes.[1] They quote the account of a member of the American force, a man named Herman Francis Reinhardt:

> The Indians were completely dumbfounded to see a lot of armed men when they expected no one and ran towards their canoes to get away. Indians knelt down on their knees and begged for life, saying that they were friends. There must have been ten or twelve killed, and that many wounded, for very few got away unhurt.

The party that headed west to Fort Hope also ran into Native people, with the same result. When the northbound force reached Fort Kamloops and met with the Hudson's Bay Company officials there, the old chief of the Shuswap Indian Band fearlessly confronted them. Chief Nicholas spoke plainly as he described the peaceful way in which both races lived together in this area. The American force broke up into smaller parties, and they continued on their way; many members were consumed with shame.

The next year saw a more peaceful arrival. A Catholic priest named Father Pandosy came into the valley in 1859 and founded a mission halfway down Okanagan Lake on the east shore. It was called simply Okanagan Mission. By 1890 there were several settlements in the valley. Enderby, located on Shuswap River, was an early one at the northern end. First known as Fortune's Landing, it was named for an early pioneer, A.L. Fortune, and was the farthest point reached by the sternwheeled steamers from Kamloops.

These pioneering watercraft were used by inveterate traveller Newton Chittenden in 1882. He gives us a charming view of this period in his *Travels in British Columbia*, and his comment on the waterborne transportation is intriguing. He writes that the vessel he used was the SS *Spallumcheen*. "The smallest of three running on the upper waters, she is not of oceanic dimensions and being built exclusively for carrying freight, her passenger accommodations are very limited." He goes on to relate that he shared a bunk with Captain Meananteu.[2]

Name changes were common. The next settlement south of Enderby was originally called Priest's Valley by another Catholic priest who came in 1862. It became Vernon in 1887 in honour of Forbes George Vernon, of whom more will be said later. Vernon was an attractive place. In 1867 a man called Cornelius O'Keefe drove a herd of cattle from Oregon Territory to a spot about nine miles north of it, where he pre-empted 162 acres of land. Within 40 years O'Keefe's holdings amounted to 15,000 acres. Of Irish descent, although from Quebec, he knew a good thing when he saw one. He built a mansion in 1880 that was still in use by his family 100 years later.

Penticton came into being at the south end of the main lake, named after a ranch belonging to the great early cattleman Tom Ellis, another Irishman. He purchased his land from the country court magistrate at Osoyoos, the renowned Judge John Carmichael Haynes, yet another Irishman, who had been one of the first border customs agents in the Interior. Haynes, who died in 1888, had mastered the art of acreage accumulation by governmental influence, and it was said he controlled almost all of the usable land from Penticton to the U.S. border. These first cattle ranchers obtained huge grants of land.

Then came Fairview, a mining camp with a suitable name but not a lasting one, and finally Osoyoos, a Native name for a settlement that had been there as early as 1862, when it was the site of a trail-side tavern. By 1890 it was said there were 400 people and 20,000 cattle in the valley. Certainly this was an exaggeration, but it was true that the raising of these beasts was the main interest of that population—although not for long. In fact, the focus was changing right then.

Forbes George Vernon added one great attribute, and here we come to our theme. He became the chief commissioner of Lands and Works in the government of Premier A.C. Elliott in 1876, and he was responsible for building roads. Initially he stayed in the job for only two years, but he came back to it in 1887, under premiers A.E.B. Davie and John Robson, and stayed for eight years, until 1895. He built some much-needed roads.

During his first stint in office Vernon completed a primitive wagon road from Kamloops to Priest's Valley, where he and his brother had a ranch, and then he extended it on to Okanagan Mission (which became Kelowna in 1892). It was rough and narrow and built to 10 feet in width (in some places, just 7), but in his second time around he widened and improved it to a standard 18-foot width. This brought him great acclaim from the residents east of the main lake, but not those west of it. They had to wait many years for a good and continuous road. They fumed as they watched the heavy wagons and stagecoaches passing freely back and forth to other areas across the lake.

On September 27, 1900, the Canadian Good Roads Association, which had been founded in 1894, held a meeting in Kamloops. Its purpose was to spread the word that the automobile had arrived and there was a great need for better roads. The Good Roads Association formed a branch in British Columbia one month later. It was first located in Vancouver and then moved to Victoria. This resulted in a spur being applied to the public works department of the western province, which finally produced a report of work needed for roads provincewide. This appeared in 1902. Things took time in those days.

The Good Roads Association reported that the road down the Okanagan Valley was almost unusable, particularly the stretch from Kaleden to Okanagan Falls. The association stated that this section was narrow, had poor alignment and contained some very steep grades. There was a map enclosed that showed no road at all for 10 miles from Deep Creek to Trout Creek on the stretch between Westbank and Penticton. In 1914 the group issued a follow-up report and map, which indicated that the road was complete from Westbank to Penticton and that $10,431.89 had been spent to relocate and rebuild the road from Kaleden to Okanagan Falls.

There was also a rather strange note: "A large overhanging rock at Vaseux Lake, which had presented a danger to the traveller, was barred from the roadway by a rock shed built in 1914." That year the report also advised us that "the Fairview-Penticton Road had grades reduced from 18 to 20 per cent to 8 per cent and was rock surfaced. Several miles were turnpiked."

So while the folks on the west side grumbled, the automobile drivers did not get off scot-free, and, as will be described later, the Westbank to Penticton road still had at least one section of nine feet in width. Even

A Wagon Road: The *Kelowna Daily Courier* of September 22, 1962, quotes a 1912 news report that described part of the old Vernon Road as "a strip of forest and quagmire." This photo was taken the same year. It is not the Vernon Road (it is the Cariboo Road), but it could be! Wagons were also using the old Vernon Road that year.

Lakeshore Road between Penticton and Summerland.

The Fairview-Penticton Road at Vaseux Lake

with the reduction of grades, the width and alignment made it very difficult to use the road to move the agricultural harvest, and travel by automobile remained an adventure for another 10 years.

Help for less adventurous travellers had come some decades earlier, when Sicamous, a small settlement on the shore of Shuswap Lake, became the starting point for a railway spur line down the valley. It was built by local residents (Moses Lumby, for whom the town was named, conceived it, and F.G. Vernon backed him) and then taken over by the Canadian Pacific Railway. Opened in 1892, it passed through Vernon on its way to Okanagan Lake. The butt of many jokes—they said you could walk the length of it faster than the train progressed, as it was constantly dropping off empty cars and picking up carloads of farm produce along the way—it was nonetheless a wonderful answer to the question of how to access this wonderful valley.

It was not a coincidence that this line ended at the lake, as lake transportation was considered an obvious method for moving people and materials right from the start. Various ferry services, initially just for passengers, had been provided on the main lake for many years by private individuals. The first of these was a real character by the name of Thomas Dolman Shorts who, in 1883, started rowing a boat around the lake, delivering people and goods, and finally graduated to a steam-powered vessel before he went off to the Klondike in 1898 and did not return. His schedule was kindly described by one of his first customers as "occasional." Shorts Point was named after him.

As more and more people arrived, along with the railway spur line, it became clear that there was no better form of transportation than the graceful steamers of the era with their large paddlewheels at the stern. The CPR promptly started building a sternwheeler at Okanagan Landing, which is what the original railway builders had named their lakeside terminus. They put a landing there, and the CPR built a depot and eventually set out more than 30 landings around the lake following the launch of its first sternwheeler, the SS *Aberdeen*, on May 22, 1893.

This vessel was named after Lord Aberdeen, and here we meet the first truly aristocratic valley family—the leader a Scotsman, the erstwhile Governor General of Canada, no less, and his graceful and intelligent Scottish wife, Lady Aberdeen, and their four children. Before we hear more about sternwheelers, let us look at the lordship and his lady. The lady is the more interesting character of the two.

The SS *Aberdeen* at Penticton. To emigrants from those parts of Britain wracked by the Industrial Revolution in the 19th century, the Okanagan Valley must have seemed like a little bit of heaven.

Short and stocky, she had already founded the Victorian Order of Nursing before she came to the Okanagan, and she was outstanding in several other ways. First and foremost, and despite being titled, she abhorred class distinction in any form. Second, she had an overwhelming desire to make the community around her new home a friendly one to live in, and she did that with her kindness and good sense. Vernon became, in one female resident's words, "a happy place to live in." Lady Aberdeen created that feeling, and it was contagious. The whole of the Okanagan Valley became a wonderful place to live. She also built a cottage hospital.

Lord Aberdeen and his family were the best influence ever to come to the Okanagan. He encouraged emigration from Britain, started a real estate boom by example, and introduced commercial fruit growing. Lady Aberdeen believed in a classless society and founded a cottage hospital in Vernon.

Lord Aberdeen was interesting too. On his first visit to B.C. he had fallen in love with the Okanagan Valley, and he followed this by becoming an ardent promoter of it, purchasing two ranches, the first of which he bought from Forbes George Vernon. After leaving his high office, Lord Aberdeen stayed on in Canada, residing in Vernon, and with the B.C. premier at the end of the century, John Herbert Turner, he started one of the greatest people-moving projects ever undertaken.

This was achieved by a well-run immigration program that brought people from Britain to British Columbia. The CPR cooperated with its transatlantic liners, cross-country railway, spur line and, finally, lake steamers comfortably carrying the new immigrants to wherever they wanted to go on the shores of Lake Okanagan. When the *Aberdeen* went into service, the provincial government chartered a service to meet it at Kelowna and transfer traffic from it across the lake. This ended up being a steam tug and barge that could carry up to three automobiles, which provided subsidized ferry service between Kelowna and Westbank from 1906 to 1927. (The sternwheelers did not regularly carry vehicles along the lakeshore. Their service was of a landing-to-landing nature.)

The *Aberdeen* acquired sister ships on the lake quite soon, with dozens of landing points served. The luxury of this service culminated in the SS *Sicamous,* a wonderful lake boat with 36 staterooms; six dining tables set with the finest linen, silver and crystal; and, rather surprisingly, space for up to 16 automobiles in its hold (this car-transporting facility was only used in the 1920s).

The sternwheelers were almost the only means of transportation serving the communities on the lake from the mid-1890s right up to the start of the First World War in 1914, which brought an end to the slow, quiet life they represented.

There was an extraordinary society in the Okanagan Valley in the decades prior to that 1914–18 war. It was almost entirely self-sufficient, certainly in the ways of entertainment and recreation. Because the newcomers were mostly British they played cricket, of course, and with horses everywhere they played polo and even rode to hounds on coyote hunts. For this they removed the top two logs of the four-log fences, and if the women, who always rode sidesaddle, could not jump a horse over two logs that way, they would not be there. One woman, reminiscing in later years, said they all had at least two horses "because there were sheep to keep, and the roads were vile." In the larger communities there was always the Saturday night dance, amazingly formal in terms of dress in these years, but still a wonderful social introducer.[3]

Many of the Okanagan residents were remittance men, a consequence of the strange English law of primogeniture in which the eldest son inherited all the wealth and, if applicable, the title. The English aristocrats of Queen Victoria's day invariably applied this statute, with disastrous effects for their daughters and younger sons.[4] While the elder son of a noble family became a viscount or an earl, the other siblings attained only a useless appendage, "The Honourable," to go before their name. (Even Winston Churchill was not exempt from this; he was related to the Duke of Marlborough, but he never used "The Honourable.")

The problem was what to do with these displaced and discontented young people. With B.C. energetically promoting emigration from Britain to the province, with an emphasis on the Okanagan, the obvious and best solution was to send them there, and they were dispatched with a monthly remittance to keep them away. They came in profusion.

As well as the remittance men there were "the Young Englishmen," males in their late teens who roamed the British Empire in these years, seeking adventure on a low budget. They found work in the Okanagan orchards at very low wages, and they augmented their diet with fish from local streams. When one shot a deer, they all feasted on venison. If they attended an Anglican Church on Sunday, they almost surely obtained an invitation to dinner that night. One who regularly rowed the length of Okanagan Lake said that the lakeshore houses were few and far between, but if he passed one at mealtime, as often as not he was asked in to join the family at the table.

It must have been a wonderful relief for many of these young men and women to experience the relative freedom of Okanagan society after coming from the rigid rules of society of the Victorian years in Britain, but many conventions persisted. The ladies' lounge, for example, included in every sternwheeler and by far the most luxuriously appointed place on board, was strictly out of bounds to members of the other sex, except for staff, at all times. Of course, such attempts to offset the course of nature were to little avail, and marriage came to many, sadly and often tragically disrupted when the peace of that world came to an end in 1914.

These British immigrants, individually different and unconventional as many of them were, had one thing in common: they were patriotic, and a touching photograph of the Okanagan's finest sternwheeler, the SS *Sicamous*, at the pier at Kelowna, bears witness to that. The photo, taken in 1914, shows the *Sicamous* about to leave with 1,000 army volunteers aboard and hundreds of supporters watching them go.

When the survivors returned, sadly fewer in number but soon joined by newer immigrants, it turned out they had different ideas in the post-war years about this old way of life with its gracious steamer travel. In 1919 they wanted cars. And for cars they needed roads, and the first

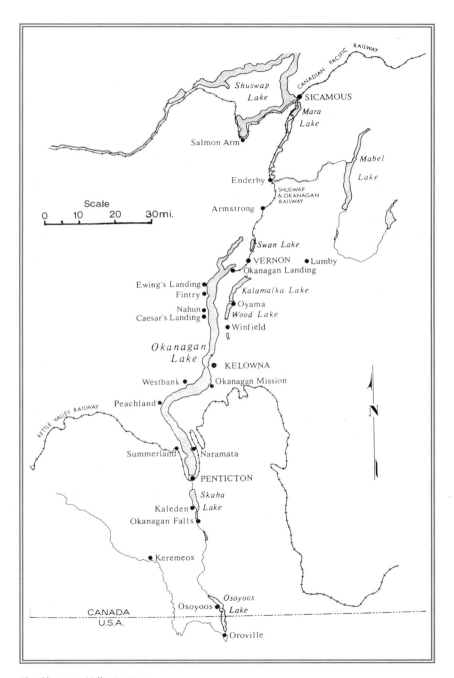

The Okanagan Valley in 1914

The SS *Sicamous* at Kelowna in 1914 with the Okanagan Valley's manpower contribution to the First World War and a good crowd of citizens to see them off.

thing desired by those people living on the west side was an adequate ferry service from Kelowna to Westbank.

Until 1927 they had to put up with the steam tug and barge, but by then traffic across the lake had increased to such an extent that the public works department went into the business itself and launched a wooden-hulled, 15-car, 94-foot-long, screw-driven ferry, the MV *Kelowna-Westbank*. In 1939 this was replaced by the ferry everyone remembers, the steel-hulled, 30-car MV *Pendozi*. The vessel was named for the first missionary in the Okanagan District (though they got the spelling wrong), and it was joined by the MV *Lequime* in 1947 and the MV *Lloyd Jones* in 1950. These three served until 1958, when they were replaced by the Okanagan Lake Bridge.[5]

In the year 1918, with the veterans back and wanting roads, we have to remember one of the most memorable district engineers that the B.C. Department of Public Works ever put before the public, one William K. Gwyer. Bill Gwyer was a civil engineer with the Canadian Northern Pacific Railway (which became the Canadian National) when the CNPR built its line through the Fraser Canyon, a task completed in

The MV *Kelowna-Westbank* was the first government-operated ferry on the Kelowna-to-Westbank run. The wooden-hulled 15-car ferry started service in 1927.

The MV *Pendozi*, named after Father Pandosy, took over from the *Kelowna-Westbank* in 1939 and gave excellent service until it was replaced by a bridge in 1958. It carried twice as many cars as its predecessor.

1915. Following this he took one of the newly created positions with the Department of Public Works as a district engineer.

Given his previous employment, he was no stranger to hard work, and he was also an excellent and imaginative civil engineer. Gwyer's problem rested with his impulsively aggressive nature, something that he never hesitated to express in words or put on paper when dealing with the public. Unfortunately we cannot now hear his words, but we can read some of his letters, as well as some of the letters that he and the department received. They are all there to see in the old Department of Public Works files.

His first task in 1918 was to report to the minister of public works, Dr. J.H. King, on whether the department should replace the Fraser Canyon road or substitute a road from Hope to Princeton. Not surprisingly, Gwyer made an excellent report. Also not surprisingly, he recommended the Canyon. His reason was that there was greater snowfall on the other route, a doubtful distinction, but more true then, when winters were harsher. (They became even harsher between 1925 and 1935, when there were only three winters that were not heavy with snow.)

Gwyer was then posted to Penticton, in charge of a large road district that included north and south Okanagan and the Similkameen area, and extended to Greenwood and on to Grand Forks. His first task, presumably of his own choosing, was to carry out a survey of the lakeshore between Penticton and Peachland in order to determine how much of the road between these points was above the high-water level of the lake. This showed his engineering sagacity; he knew this was vital information that he had to have.

His survey revealed that 11 of the 26 miles were within six feet or less of the lake level at that time. As the survey was done in February, the lake must have been near its low-water level. This was bad news because several of the extreme high-water levels reached in the past had been marked, and annual flooding was indicated.

The road had come into being incrementally, in sections spreading out upstream and downstream from the various steamboat landings. These sections were all built on relatively flat areas, usually at creek mouths or deltas close to the water's edge, and all of them were surrounded by higher land. Connecting them had been, and was to be, very difficult because the terrain consisted of a series of creek valleys, steep-sided in many places, that stretched back up the hillside. Close to Penticton there was also a problem with silty soils. This road, and the challenge to flood-proof it and to improve it generally, turned out to be a major preoccupation for Gwyer throughout his stay in Penticton from 1918 to 1927. He was only moderately successful in meeting the challenge due to a serious lack of funds and, of course, the forces of nature. However, these problems were exacerbated by the actions of a federal government civil servant, which will be described shortly.

Excerpts from letters found in the old public works files give us an insight into Gwyer's troubles from the very start. The first is from N.S. Davidson of Idylwylde Ranch, Trepanier, to Dr. King, minister of public works, dated January 16, 1919:

> I would like to draw your attention to a piece of very bad road, in fact it is dangerous to drive on. Autos come along and drive the poor devils either into Okanagan Lake or into the ditch.
>
> Some few years ago the old McBride Bowser Party undertook to give us a good road around the west side of the Okanagan from Penticton to Westbank Ferry, and the present single track trail full of devilish holes is the result.
>
> Several autos have smashed up in collision around the sharp corners between Peachland and Penticton, the distance is about 20 miles and curves amount to 162, and 21 of these are certainly dangerous. I purchased a car this fall, and now I find it a dangerous article to run, and I rather wish someone else had it. I paid $20 for the right to run it on these hellish trails. I came here fifteen years ago, and we had better roads then than we have today.

Gwyer received a copy of this epistle from the minister and he reported, in part, as follows:

> I was at first distressed at this communication—as this is our Show Road (as it were), being the main trunk route from Kamloops. I am however advised by Mr. McAlpine [the road foreman] that the portions more complained of are under the jurisdiction of the Summerland and Peachland Municipalities.

This shifted the responsibility quite nicely, but Gwyer then spoils it all with his last paragraph:

> In this respect I venture to suggest that as Mr. Davidson is learning to drive a new car, he probably requires more room than the ordinary traveler.

Dr. King, being the fine man that he was, probably took this in the right way. Later Gwyer wrote to his minister again, when he was again under heavy fire:

> I do not think that I would pay much attention to any adverse criticism, either from newspapers or from individuals. There is really so little for them to find fault with in my district that it is expected that certain factions would take every possible chance to criticize, and to blame the department for any occurrence, whether we are to blame or not.

One cannot but admire his fortitude. In another letter, to a foreman in this case, Gwyer responds to a newspaper report with a reflection on the department's lack of funds:

> Of course we do not take any notice of these articles—which emanate from the brains of feeble-minded persons, who expect Engineers to build permanent roads on wind.[6]

A sideline to all of this is a report by Gwyer in the files advising that, following the letter from Davidson, his assistant attended a protest meeting at Peachland. As the road was in very poor condition, he could not drive in and had to go there by boat! Further on in this file is a report that says some of this road was no more than nine feet wide. Anyone, not only a person just learning to drive, might need more width than that.

The federal civil servant referred to earlier was the superintendent of the Dominion Experimental Farm, which was located a few miles north of Penticton. He was seemingly as aggressive in nature as Gwyer. The farm was on a piece of land now subdivided and called Sage Mesa.

It consists of a silt bench heavily incised by natural erosion. In Gwyer's time, irrigation to promote fruit growing was the coming thing, and the superintendent went to great lengths to out-irrigate everyone—with disastrous results. The constant watering supersaturated the soil and caused land slippage and mud slides, which all ended up on Gwyer's road at the lakeside below the mesa. This started in the early 1920s, and Gwyer's letters about the situation, to the superintendent and then to Ottawa, would be a good way to start a war.

In the first place, Gwyer showed none of the respect the Dominion government expected from lesser authorities in those days. Most of the confrontation was on the phone, but there is a 1927 letter from the experimental farm superintendent denying any responsibility and suggesting the province relocate the road at its own expense. Gwyer replied to this in a letter on September 27, 1927. "There is not the slightest hope of the Department abandoning the lower road. A bill will be submitted to you covering the total expense incurred this year in opening the road. I have decided to forget the expense incurred last year." It was quite enough for those in Ottawa to write off the Okanagan!

The superintendent vociferously denied starting anything. Fortunately it all commenced just before Gwyer's departure, as his successor, the engineer from Prince Rupert with whom Gwyer exchanged places, was a better man to write to the senior government than Gwyer was.

This is a 1980 view of the West Side Road at the "bottleneck" near Nahun. It stayed that bad for a long time.

Sage Mesa, a few miles north of Penticton, was the former site of the Dominion Experimental Farm. Over-irrigation led to land slippage and mud slides.

Much later, a detailed soil survey showed that the excess water migrated to the face of the bluff, and that caused the slides.

Twenty-five major slides occurred over 20 years, and road closures of two to three weeks' duration were not unusual. The farm disappeared after some years, and less irrigation slowed the problem, but it still exists. One positive result was that the huge amount of silt and other soils running out into the lake created shallows, which made it possible to move the road out into the lake on a rock fill for part of its length, after the lake bottom had been stabilized.

Experience has shown that when it comes to transportation and politics in British Columbia, and Canada, there are seldom any coincidences. It might have seemed a coincidence that for so many years there was no viable through road on the west side of the lake from Westbank north, and that the poor condition of the road when it was connected was one of the main reasons the orchardists persisted in shipping their produce by steamer, but it is almost certain that it was not coincidental. Forbes George Vernon had favoured the residents of the east side with a good 18-foot-wide road from Vernon to Kelowna in the late 1800s, but there was no patron to provide that on the west side.

Goodbye, Gwyer

As politicians and civil servants well know, the public has its preferences, and sometimes it is remarkably obtuse in pursuing them. The fruit growers of the Okanagan Valley were most proud of their experimental farm as a symbol of their maturity. Bill Gwyer's public criticism of the superintendent was a political embarrassment, and those in charge in Ottawa and Victoria knew what to do about that—transfer him (the method of dealing with difficult district engineers since the position was first created).

He was transferred to Prince Rupert District in 1927. In his last report on his Okanagan work he talks about experimenting with tarvia throughout Penticton municipality, an experiment that would not work out. He was a strange man and one who was always experimenting.

At Prince Rupert he decided to carry out an aerial survey between that city and Terrace to find a different route for the road, as he believed he could get through by way of two Interior valleys instead of along the Skeena River. Considering that in the 1920s there were very few aircraft capable of operating at a level higher than many of these peaks, and that it was cloudy most of the time in the area, this was a courageous initiative. He did it, though, and the bids on it and the reports in the files are interesting, but there was no pass, and he had to drop the idea.

Gwyer was often taken away from his district to be used on highway location work, and in the summer and fall of 1933 he headed a location survey for the Tolmie government on the proposed route for a trans-Canada highway between Revelstoke and Golden, the Big Bend highway. He worked very hard and for very long hours on this as Tolmie wanted a complete survey before the election which, due to the five-year limit, he had to call for November of that year.

The Big Bend highway was a shared project with the Dominion government. The province had done almost nothing on its section from Revelstoke to Boat Encampment under Tolmie, while the Canada Parks Department people had gone ahead steadfastly with their half, from the mid-point to Golden.

Gwyer got the survey completed, and he received much praise from the deputy minister, Pat Philip, but it did neither him nor the government any good. The Tolmie government lost all its seats but one. We see nothing further of W.K. Gwyer in the annual reports or in the files, and the reports from a few years later indicate there was a different engineer at Prince Rupert. This is one more reason to deplore the total destruction of all the old Department of Public Works personnel records in the 1950s.

In the mid-1920s the residents between Penticton and Westbank, in their despair, went to Richard Marpole, the CPR superintendent in Vancouver, and asked him to use his influence to get them a good road. It was no coincidence that he did not see his way clear to help them. The railway company, not surprisingly, did not support better roads. Instead, in 1923 the CPR opened a line from Penticton to Osoyoos, with rail barge service for a portion of it along Skaha Lake until that water trip was replaced by rail in 1931. This provided rail freight service from the south to Penticton, where the Kettle Valley Railway, a CPR associate, could move it either east or west.

When the Canadian National Railway opened a line from Kamloops to Kelowna in 1925, it was a major blow to the request for a west-shore road as it overcame both congestion on the old CPR line and the CPR monopoly, generally making rail transport more feasible. Amazingly, this nationally owned railway did not receive permission from Ottawa to carry passengers until 1935—when the CPR took it over.[7]

In 1935, the proponents of the beloved SS *Sicamous* arranged for the Canadian taxpayer to pay a large annual subsidy to keep the steamer parting the lake waters in lieu of a road, but the very next year all concerned realized it was a lost cause, and the beloved vessel was tied up for the last time, soon to be moved onto land and displayed as a tourist attraction, which it still is today.

Road improvements continued through the 1940s, and the final improvement, making the road from Penticton to Westbank two lanes, was completed, as described in the Minister of Highways Report for 1956, after W.A.C. Bennett had been helping greatly by supporting it:

> Nearly all work done was on uncompleted contracts from last year. Twenty-two miles were completed this year, and one contract was let and started at Powers Creek.

Four-laning was started in one non-urban area in 1981, and it happened to be the same stretch of road that had plagued Bill Gwyer 55 years earlier when it was all of nine feet wide.

This project, 2.3 miles from Westbank to Kelowna, was built be-tween October 1, 1981, and November 15, 1982 (eight months ahead of schedule), and it cost $7 million, including land purchase. Such a figure for that mileage would have been unimaginable to Gwyer (the total capital roads program for B.C. in 1926 was just under $2 million), as would the width of the roadway, 68 feet, and the capacity of the highway for up to 4,000 cars an hour, averaging 30,000 vehicles a day. It met another section to the south to make a total of five miles at that standard.

This high-capacity highway brought the shortcomings of the two-lane Okanagan Lake Bridge to the forefront. Because its deck was 36 feet wide, it could feasibly contain three 12-foot lanes without

A view of the Okanagan Lake Bridge, which was opened by HRH Princess Margaret in 1958. The crossing is 1, 675 yards long, with structure for 800 yards and a roadway width of 12 yards. Originally a two-lane bridge, it was converted in 1984 to three lanes, with the centre lane made reversible by traffic control lights.

shoulders, instead of the existing two lanes with 6-foot shoulders. The decision was made to convert it, with reversible traffic flow in the centre lane using traffic control lights. This went into effect in 1984, and at the same time the anchors and anchor cables to the six floating sections were replaced.

An American engineer who worked on the floating bridge in Seattle gave an interesting opinion about the safety of this bridge when he was asked if he would participate in its original design in the 1950s. He declined on the basis of the hazard he considered to exist from floating ice at the site. He doubtless knew of the events of the winter of 1949–50, when ice formed on the lake to a thickness of eight inches. When the ice cover broke up, a large floe moved downstream, swung around as it passed the Kelowna ferry landing, and slightly damaged both the piling and the ferry that was tied up there. (Ninety years earlier, in the 1860s, John Allison (of Allison Pass), an early cattleman at Westbank, was almost killed when his rowboat was crushed between two ice floes in this vicinity.)

The Difference of 40 Years: The upper photo is of the Okanagan Highway nine miles south of Vernon alongside Kalamalka Lake. It was taken in 1942. The surface looks like a recently applied spray of liquid asphalt covered with sand, which was usually applied twice, an improvement over loose gravel that was very popular at the time. Unfortunately, most of these surfaces came apart in the severe frost breakup of the spring of 1943 in the Interior. The plant mix pavement shown in the lower photo of the Penticton Channel Parkway, taken in the early 1980s, is able to withstand the effects of frost for many years.

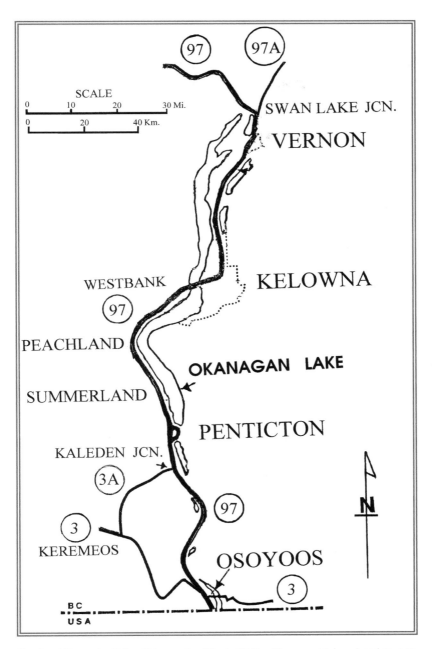

The Road Down the Valley: This map is of Route 97 (the Okanagan Highway) and its main connecting highways as they were at the end of the 1980s. Shown here is the portion from Swan Lake Junction to the U.S. border, some 119 miles.

In only one year since then has there been ice of similar thickness, but no damage was inflicted, and global warming lessens concerns for the future. Fortunately for the people of Kelowna, the highway department was willing to take a chance in the mid-1950s and built the bridge.

The opening of the Penticton Channel Parkway, a total bypass of the city centre, on July 13, 1984, added to the multi-laning of the highway along the main lake. This was followed in October 1990 by the completion of the Okanagan Connector, a link to the Coquihalla Highway from Hope, which came in north of Peachland and forever changed the nature of traffic on the west side and, some think, of the valley itself.

Things have changed, but the beauty of the lake and its valley has remained constant.

CHAPTER 2

THE ROAD UP THE LAKE

The earth's bounty brought miners to the shores of Kootenay Lake and steamboats to its waters. The settlers, who followed reluctantly, finally gained a lakeshore road of character.

*T*his next story about a road in a valley alongside a lake is set about 130 miles east of the one just described, and it shows the remarkable difference in development around two similar natural features when British Columbia's mountainous terrain demands it. Okanagan Lake is removed from the mountains by some miles, while Kootenay Lake is totally within them, in a trench separating the Purcell Range from the Selkirks. This variation in surrounding terrain resulted in a profound difference, not only in the topography of the lakeshore, but also in the timing, extent and nature of the early lakeside settlement.

Kootenay Lake is about 20 percent larger than Okanagan Lake, and it is arguably just as beautiful, although in a different way, with its substantial edging of mountains on either side. It lacks cultivable land around it, except for the flats at the head of the lake (which are 3 miles wide and 25 miles long). Its shores are steep and rocky, and usable land is confined to the outflow deltas of the many streams, mostly small and steep, which flow into it. There is more usable land on the north shore of the lake's West Arm and at the end of that arm on the south shore (where the city of Nelson lies), although both areas are far from flat.[1]

This view of B.C. mountains shows rather neatly the difference between those below 4,266 feet and those above. The former were rounded off by the Arctic ice cap that moved into and out of B.C., the last time 10,000 years ago. The mountains in the background are above 4,266 feet and are as originally formed, except for erosion and gouging caused by the alpine glaciation of the ice age. The mountains around Okanagan Lake are within the intermontane system known as the Okanagan Highlands, and are all below 4,266 feet and rounded. The mountains around Kootenay Lake are in the Cassiar-Columbia Mountains, where peaks over 4,266 feet are rugged and sharp-edged.

How does the history of transportation around Kootenay Lake differ from that around Okanagan Lake? For one thing, it happened much later. By 1902, the road down the Okanagan Valley was almost complete, except for the stretch from Peachland to Summerland. In contrast, in that year the only roads in the East Kootenay existed around Cranbrook and Fernie, and in the West Kootenay there were no trunk roads at all—simply access roads to lake and railway centres.

This belated road development was due to variations in settlement in the two regions. In 1879, when B.C. was in a recession just prior to the commencement of the construction of the CPR, there was at least the beginning of a cattle-raising community in the Okanagan Valley. This included such ranchers as Cornelius O'Keefe, who arrived in 1867, Tom Ellis (1869) and Price Ellison (1876), and, of course, pioneers Forbes George Vernon and John Allison before them. In those years, farming and orchard cultivation were also gradually spreading south from Shuswap Lake. According to the B.C. Sessional Papers for 1874, in that year 91 cattle ranchers in Kamloops and the Nicola and Okanagan valleys signed a petition for a direct road from Merritt to Hope. (They got a trail.) This did not indicate many residents, but it was a good start for an occupational community. In comparison, in the East Kootenay area the total non-Native population in 1882 was reported as being no more than 11.

Population began to increase in the Kootenays between 1882 and 1893, after the discovery of rich silver and lead deposits, mostly close to Kootenay Lake.[2] Almost all the new residents came from the south, and they were often transient, as mining people usually were. Rail lines and water transport followed that industry instead of roads.

The first vessel on the lake to move people and goods was a steam launch of no great size, the *Midge*, brought out from England in the 1880s by William Adolf Baillie-Grohman to help in his land reclamation project on the river at Creston (see chapter 6). This boat was piloted by Charlie Davis, who also grew vegetables on the flats and ran a grocery delivery service to points on the lake between Creston and Nelson. Davis and the *Midge* both disappeared with the 1894 flood: Davis left the area and the *Midge* sank. It was resurrected from its resting place on the river bottom at Bonners Ferry, Idaho, but it did not last long, sinking again at West Creston.

Another waterborne service was established when Jim Hill, president of the Great Northern Railway, rented the sternwheeler SS *Nelson* from the Columbia and Kootenay Steam Navigation Company in the early 1890s. He used it to haul ore from the Slocan mines (north of Kaslo) up Kootenay Lake and River to Bonners Ferry. Fortunately the *Nelson* had an exceptionally powerful engine (from the old Fraser River boat SS *Skuzzy*), which allowed it to make its way against the strong

The steam launch *Midge*, with its teak hull, was brought from England by ship and train to Sandpoint, Idaho, then manhandled to Bonners Ferry, with the help of pulleys, tackle and log rollers. In the background are the Creston Flats.

current. It delivered materials and produce from Bonners Ferry on the return trip.

The mining works of interest in the Kootenays were at Ainsworth and at Riondel. The latter was the site of the large and rich Bluebell Mine, which was staked in 1882. After a claim-jumping that led to a murder,[3] it became the property of Captain George J. Ainsworth, an American who was the early promoter of the Columbia and Kootenay Steam Navigation Company, the forerunner of the CPR lake service. He founded his namesake town across the lake from the future location of Riondel in 1887. Ainsworth was originally established to take advantage of the nearby hot springs, but it got its own mine two years later. It lost its prominence as the region's largest settlement when Kaslo got the railway terminal.

In 1895, mining interests in the area decided to build a smelter for their ore. The Pilot Bay smelter, located at a small bay about eight miles south of Riondel, cost the astounding sum, for those years, of $650,000. Unfortunately for the investors, their foresight was faulty. The smelter stayed in production for only a few years and lay idle after America's Great Northern Railway and its vessels departed in 1910, which ended the movement of ore southwards. The smelter's stacks and walls remained for decades as a memento of turn-of-the-century mining madness.

A French company bought the Bluebell Mine in 1905, and the town beside it was named for the company president. (The road to Riondel from Kootenay Bay did not appear until much later.)

Not all settlement on the shores of Kootenay Lake was connected with mining. The area south of Pilot Bay on the east side became a resting place for remittance men, mostly from England, the majority of whom arrived in the last decade of the 19th century. Unlike the Okanagan, which was the choice of most remittance men, the Kootenays did not offer the option of growing fruit for a living. Settlement sites alongside Kootenay Lake were too small in area, too few and too isolated to permit living off the land. To settle there you had to have financial support (to fill the larder) as well as an adventurous nature (to enjoy the isolation). Beauty and tranquility were offered and easily claimed, and many of those who put down roots there felt they had achieved their own particular paradise. This was reflected in the names they gave their heart's content—Destiny Bay being a typical example.

Wheeling and Dealing

In 1891, Eli Carpenter discovered a rich silver deposit in the Slocan district and established the Payne Mine, which paid out the highest dividends of any underground operation in British Columbia for many years. The story is that he and a companion became so frustrated at their lack of success prospecting in the Slocan Valley that they decided to go back to their hotel room in Ainsworth as quickly as possible, directly across the mountains, and there they found the precious ore. Carpenter was a circus acrobat and tightrope walker, and when the new railway and the new sternwheeler met in Slocan City in July 1897, he took part in the town's gala day by walking a high wire across the main street, pushing a wheelbarrow. He was not successful in getting any of his friends to ride with him. Those were the days!

Carpenter was a wheeler-dealer of the old style, and they named a creek after him, which was placed in a culvert down the centre of the main street of Sandon. Carpenter Creek went on a rampage in a flood many years later and washed out most of the buildings in town, but it did not matter because by then the town was dead.

In 1882, Robert Evan Sproule staked a very rich galena ledge, which he named the Bluebell, at a location that later became the townsite of Riondel. Unfortunately, he could not reach a claim recorder in the minimum time, and Thomas Hammil recorded the claim for himself. Sproule's court action was overturned by an appeal, and he became incensed and killed Hammil by gunshot. He was tried, convicted of murder and hanged. The highly valued claim went to Hammil's employer, George J. Ainsworth and his associates.

A creek near Nelson was named for Sproule, which showed that the public was probably on his side, but the name has other prominence in the memories of long-time residents of Nelson. It was at the Sproule Creek School that Wesley Black, the MLA, held a public meeting to discuss the Doukhobor problem early in the 1950s. He told the Doukhobors that they would all go to jail if they persisted in keeping their children out of school. Thereupon all the Doukhobor women present at the meeting, including some of great age, silently and steadfastly removed all their clothing in protest. Most of the non-Doukhobor men present went into deep shock, and it was a long time before Wes Black got over that.[4]

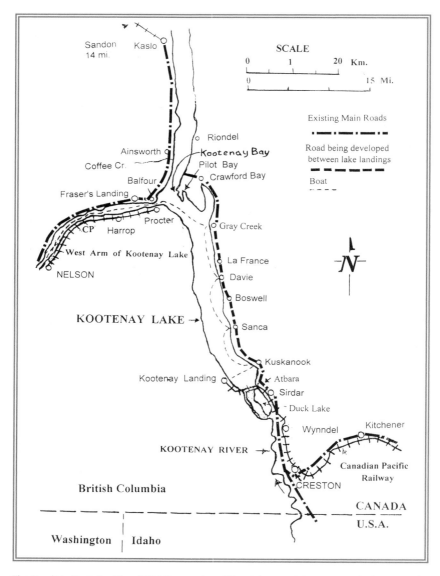

The Road Up the Lake, Circa 1927: Ainsworth and Riondel were mining centres; the latter was the site of the rich Bluebell Mine. As a result of the mining boom in the Kootenays, a railway arrived at the head of Kootenay Lake in 1898. (Note: Destiny Bay is located between Boswell and Sanca.)

As a result of the mining boom in the Kootenays, a railway arrived at the head of Kootenay Lake, from Crowsnest Pass and Alberta, in 1898 (see chapter 3). Discouraged by the difficulty of continuing along the mountainous western shore from Kootenay Landing to Procter, the Canadian Pacific Railway delayed this final link, and nothing happened for 32 years. Train barges and tugs filled the gap, and a dependable delivery service for people and goods was provided by the numerous steamers plying the lake. They seldom went directly to Nelson, but dropped in at many small landings on either side of the lake along the way. After *Midge* and *Nelson* came the SS *Moyie* (which began providing service for passengers and freight in 1898 and continued until 1957), the SS *Kuskanook* (which entered service in 1906) and, on April 30, 1913, the most luxurious sternwheeler of them all, the SS *Nasookin*. Water was the only way in. No one worried about the problem of eventually joining up these properties along the rocky shores by road because everyone thought the lake steamers would be there forever. Unfortunately they were not, although the steamers on the Arrow and Kootenay lakes lasted much longer than those farther west due to the effort required to build roads to replace them.

The difficult nature of road building in the Kootenays was recognized by the provincial road authority in 1902 when it ruled that all trunk roads in the province had to be at least 10 to 14 feet wide, but those in the Kootenays could be 9 feet wide. This was readily accepted because the mines shipped out by water, and residents had the fine lake steamers to serve them.

At some point in the early 1900s, a primitive road was built from Crawford Bay to Kootenay Bay and later extended south to Grey's Creek (regrettably changed later by map-makers to Gray Creek). This road was, of course, no wider than nine feet. A through road from Gray Creek to Kuskanook was not completed until the 1930s.

In 1909, when users of the newly popular automobile demanded that a road from the Lower Mainland to the Interior be created *somewhere*, B.C.'s premier Richard McBride gave the assignment to his minister of public works, Thomas "Good Roads" Taylor.[5] Taylor decided to start work on a southern route, first from Hope to Princeton, and then on through Osoyoos to Nelson and farther east, including, of course, the

56-mile ferry trip between Nelson and Kuskanook (though there were plans to shorten this leg of the journey).

Taylor failed to connect Hope and Princeton, but the idea of a southern route remained, and after the road through the Fraser Canyon was restored during the term of Premier John Oliver in the mid-1920s, a winding trans-provincial alternative came to pass. It stretched from Hope to Spences Bridge, then on to Merritt, and from there via Princeton to Osoyoos, Nelson, Fernie and the Crowsnest Pass. This long way across the province by road was finally shortened when the Hope-Princeton Highway opened in 1949, and it was one of only two roads to Alberta in those days, along with the route from Cranbrook through Radium to Vermilion Pass.

We are indebted to an old Department of Public Works road file for a revealing account of a trans-provincial odyssey in the late 1920s.[6] It takes the form of a bulletin dated June 1, 1927, issued by the Automobile Club of Southern California. This historic document describes a trip some American visitors made by car, using the newly opened Fraser Canyon Highway and then proceeding eastwards through Kamloops and Penticton and on to Nelson and Crowsnest Pass. Of the section of this trip from Osoyoos to Cranbrook, 275 miles, the bulletin says:

> Turning easterly a fair sandy road climbs over Anarchist Mountain, (elevation 3800 ft.), thence fair to good natural gravel down through Kettle Valley to Midway. The same type of road winds through easy grades through a mountainous country to Grand Forks and Cascade from where good two-lane natural gravel road is used to Rossland and Trail, thence along the Kootenay River [sic—it is the Columbia River] where a free government ferry is used to cross the Columbia River. The same type of good natural gravel is then used to Nelson where it is necessary to ferry Kootenay Lake to Kuskanook Landing. The ferry leaves Nelson daily at 6.30 a.m., and leaves Kuskanook daily at 4.10 p.m. The charges are from $5.00 to $7.00 according to the size of the car, and $2.20 per passenger. From Kuskanook Landing a fair natural gravel road is traversed via Creston to Yahk with good gravel to Cranbrook.[7]

William Ramsay was the district engineer at Nelson in 1927, and he must have been delighted with the restrained wording of this bulletin when it reached him, knowing as he did the real condition of some sections of these roads (see the map Bill Ramsay's District in chapter 4). The description "good two-lane natural gravel road" will certainly raise the eyebrows of anyone who drove from Cascade to Rossland even as recently as the 1940s and 1950s. For one thing, this "good two-lane road" went plumb through the centre of a mining operation a few miles out of Rossland, and there was barely 10 yards of space between the buildings. For "natural gravel" read "egg size and larger" or just "bare rock," and gravel or not, it often became impassible in the spring or in periods of heavy rain or snow. It would have been better to substitute for "fair" the word "challenging," and the condition described elsewhere in the bulletin as "poor when wet" was perhaps a polite way of saying "worse than deplorable."

In view of the constantly poor condition of this crossing of the Monashee Range, most travellers preferred to go south at Cascade, cross the Columbia River at Northport, Washington, and come back into Canada at Waneta. The old Cascade-Rossland roadway, which included two summits, had to be experienced to be believed, especially when one was travelling in the Greyhound bus, which had to stay on the Canadian side of the border and could not make many of the curves in one try. The opening of the Christina Lake to Castlegar route in 1962 was a great relief. The old road remained a challenge until it was closed in 1966.

The long-lasting train-ferry trip passed into history when the CPR finally opened its missing railway link along the west side of Kootenay Lake in December 1930. The need for lake transport—tugs and barges and a sternwheeler to transport rail passengers—disappeared overnight. As a result, the CPR first leased out and then sold the grand old *Nasookin* to the Department of Public Works as a ferry. This was the government's stopgap solution to its failure to provide a fully connected road along the east shore.

The *Nasookin* continued to make two round trips a day, starting from Fraser's Landing instead of Nelson, which cut 20 miles from the trip to Kuskanook. Of course this could not last. The old sternwheeler's wooden hull had endured well beyond the normal lifespan of such vessels in similar waters,[8] and it was not logical to replace one many-hours-long ferry trip with another at this late date. The situation could only be resolved by making a continuous route out of the various road sections that existed at all the landings from Gray Creek to Kuskanook. This, in turn, would make possible a shorter lake crossing from Gray Creek to Fraser's Landing, a ferry trip of about 10 miles in length.

There was, however, one large problem in building roads in British Columbia from 1930 onwards. It was called the Great Depression, and it was responsible for a total lack of capital funding for highway construction for many years, particularly in the early 1930s. These were the years of the relief camps operated by the Canadian army and

The SS *Nasookin* before the change. In this form it was licensed to carry 350 passengers.

The SS *Nasookin* at Nelson after one full deck and the rear half of the top deck were removed.

the Department of Public Works. Ultimately the army took over all
the camps, using provincial public works equipment, but with DPW
personnel as onlookers only.

Relief workers started off in 1931 to join up the sections of road
on the east shore, and the Annual Report of the Department of Public
Works for that year tells us:

> Between Creston and Kuskanook the road was considerably improved,
> and three miles of the Kuskanook-Gray Creek section were completed
> to standard, thus enabling a ferry service to be inaugurated between
> Gray Creek and Fraser's Landing, and establishing a very improved
> highway connection between Nelson and the Alberta boundary via
> the Crowsnest Pass.

This was signed by P. Philip, chief engineer, as there was no deputy
minister at the time. Philip carried out those duties and was an excellent
deputy minister, one of the best in fact.[9] He went on to describe the
process involved in upgrading and completing the road, which gives us
some valuable insight into those troubled times:

> Arising out of the negotiations between the Dominion and the Province
> was the decision that many of the destitute single men should be
> provided with employment on Provincial highways, and, as a means to
> this end the erection of camps in small units capable of housing fifty to
> one hundred men each was decided upon; in a remarkably short period
> of time camps were erected at points where they would be best situated
> for the furtherance of necessary construction or reconstruction on trunk
> and selected main highways. In constructing these camps the work
> alone provided employment for 3000 men; a large volume of secondary
> employment was also created in supplying lumber, materials, etc.

The next year's report confirms the ferry going in from Gray Creek
and praises the good work of "Provincial relief workers," distinct from
"Dominion relief workers." Finally the report reads:

> The Province has in operation near Sirdar a camp for married
> men working in lieu of direct relief, and during the past fiscal year

1.1 miles of standard road in heavy side-hill country has been completed, including the replacement of 160 feet of trestle by culvert and fill amounting to 16,000 cubic yards. [Obviously these men needed a more permanent camp as their wives and children often accompanied them.]

When reading Bill Ramsay's Nelson district reports, it is not long before one realizes that he favoured the work of the married men he supervised over that of the single workers looked after by the army.

Eventually the crew at Sirdar moved north, living in tent camps in the summer months with families tenting nearby. These camps were spaced three miles apart, and the road improvements progressed north from Sirdar. One of the worst sections was from Atbara to Kuskanook, and it remained very rough for many years. As it had formerly been a railway grade, the locals liked to say with a chuckle that the Department of Public Works forgot to take out the ties when they took it over as a road.

The road improvement continued in 1934, and in 1935 the crews turned their attention to the stretch from Crawford Bay to Gray Creek, where a 1,500-foot section through heavy rock was widened by relief workers. The next year they went to the other end and widened the rocky road from Kuskanook to Atbara. (This was also the year a large farm at Crawford Bay came to international prominence because of a hen that set a world record for annual egg production, laying 337 eggs in one year.[10]) Following this, gravelling was the road crews' main operation until 1942, when the war closed down the work.

Through these years, the wonderful old *Nasookin* kept on going. In 1934 the second and third decks were removed, greatly increasing its load-carrying capacity. This was given as up to 30 cars, and it also carried the Greyhound bus, which parked across its foredeck. When not carrying the bus, the steamer could substitute the Nelson-Creston freight truck. That truck service was a wonderful aid to life in general for all east-shore residents for many years.

Although it could take 30 cars, the average car load over the years never exceeded six per trip. In 1936 it had another complete overhaul, and in 1941 it was hauled out again as its hull required strengthening.

In its absences the SS *Moyie* took over, pushing a rail transfer barge. During the war years, the ferry ran on the winter schedule (two round trips a day instead of three) all year round. The *Nasookin* retired in 1947 when the MV *Anscomb* arrived, which was a great relief because the older vessel was near the end of its life. The *Anscomb*, a fine diesel-powered ferry, could carry 40 cars and 150 passengers. In later years it was joined by a second ferry on the run, the MV *Balfour* (with a capacity of 35 cars and 150 passengers), and finally, following the retirement of the *Anscomb*, the MV *Osprey 2000* (80 cars and 250 passengers) came on the route.

The *Balfour* can claim the dubious distinction of being the only ferry to travel south on the main lake from the West Arm since that route was plied by the *Nasookin*. The vessel was powered by two Z-drive power units, one on either side at the stern, and during some of the more violent storms on the lake, the crew found that when one of these power units broke down, the *Balfour* could not come up into the wind. On one occasion this happened halfway between Balfour and Kootenay Bay. The ferry lost forward tracking motion and went south for quite a way, beam on to the wind, before the crew was able to anchor in a sheltered bay and make repairs. Later a third engine and propeller were installed on the *Balfour*'s centreline to avoid a repeat performance.

This view of the MV *Anscomb* on Kootenay Lake near Balfour was taken in 1947, on one of the first trips the vessel made across the lake in 57 years of service. The Purcell Mountains are in the background. In 1892 a rancher from Toby Creek, near Invermere, drove a herd of cattle over these mountains to feed the miners at Riondel, a mine site on the shoreline behind the ferry.

When the war ended in 1945, a contract was let for a new road that ran 7.5 miles from Gray Creek to the new ferry terminal at Kootenay Bay. It was completed, along with the terminal, in time for the *Anscomb* to commence service early in 1947. That year also saw a complete gravelling of the 26.4 miles from Gray Creek to Kuskanook prior to paving. Another 21.9 miles were paved from Kootenay Bay south to Destiny Bay.

The year 1948 brought the worst flood in British Columbia's history since 1894. The newly improved road alongside the river from Wynndel to Creston was totally inundated for many weeks when the Creston Flats flooded. To maintain traffic, the single-lane high road above the tracks was hurriedly widened to two lanes and put into service.

A year later this new route was favoured as the final one, and a contract was let for construction of a 6.25-mile highway from Creston to Wynndel. This new and higher-standard section of Highway 3 effectively permitted drivers to travel at 70 miles per hour (although such speeds were illegal at the time). In 1949 this new route and the road from Destiny Bay to Kuskanook were paved during a summer that saw the successful completion of the largest paving program ever carried out in the province.

Now Kootenay residents could drive along their lakeshore in comfort and safety and enjoy the 10-mile ferry trip from Kootenay Bay

In this photo of the highway after it was reconstructed in 1949, taken about three miles north of Creston, the Selkirk Mountains can be seen on the west side of the lake.

to Balfour. The scenery was unmatched, the road was smooth and, best of all, the ferry trip was free. Many Americans from nearby states soon appeared in the summer months as tourists to enjoy this provincial benevolence.

Residents and visitors on the West Arm also had an improved and paved road, a far cry from the obstacle that confronted earlier lakeside dwellers who wanted to drive from Balfour to Kaslo on the western shore of the main lake in the early 1920s. The DPW Annual Report of 1924 includes a map that shows a road along the lakeshore to Kaslo, but there is a gap south of Ainsworth at a point known as the Coffee Creek bluffs. Apparently this was connected soon afterwards, as shown on the map in the 1927 Annual Report.

However, the bluffs continued to be a problem for many years due to their steepness. In winter the snow would break away in huge snow-balls and roll down on the road, and in spring there were mudslides. This narrow and unreliable road was considered to be one of the main reasons the SS *Moyie* stayed in service for so many years on the Kaslo to Procter run, carrying general freight as well as rail cars.

The road up the east side of the lake had its challenges as well, but, probably thanks to its winding nature and the low speed limit of those days (with an even lower speed on curves), it did not rack up many serious motor vehicle accidents throughout the years, and few of the ones that did occur were fatal. Department of Highways people like to think this was the result of the tender care the road received from the maintenance crew at Boswell. Be that as it may, what could have been the worst accident in terms of fatalities, but luckily ended with no deaths, happened early in the 1950s.

In the middle of winter there was a mild spell overnight. Heavy rain fell on the packed snow of the lakeshore road, with the disastrous result of water on ice. This was before the days of radio-controlled overhead signs that warn of poor conditions, and all that Bill Thompson, the road foreman at Boswell, could do was turn his crew out at first light and sand steadily from his base northwards, hoping to meet the early morning Greyhound bus from Nelson before it got into trouble.

He almost made it, but minutes before he got to the bus, it met a large truck on a narrow icy section near La France Creek. As the driver tried to avoid a collision, the bus left the road and slid over a small cliff, landing on its side in waist-deep lake water. Seconds later the road crew arrived and they, with other travellers, scrambled down the cliff and helped the few passengers and stunned bus driver out of the water. In some cases this was no easy task.

Bill Thompson saw to an elderly woman who sustained a back injury and whose scalp was torn. She could not be moved, so he applied a dressing to her injury and held her out of the freezing water, which meant he was mostly standing in it, for almost an hour before the ambulance arrived. When Thompson finally climbed back up to the road, soaked to the skin, he endured a torrent of verbal abuse handed out by a local insurance adjuster, presumably because the road was not sanded earlier. Such were the trials and tribulations of maintaining the inadequate roads of these years with the very limited resources available.

Bill was a descendant of the early lakeshore community and was highly respected by all along the lake throughout his service. Always interesting, that community also contained the Honourable Basil Aylmer, for many years the well-regarded chief purser of the MV *Anscomb*. Just before his retirement, Basil could have assumed the title of Lord Aylmer on the death of his elder brother in England, but he never did.

The early name of Grey's Creek is intriguing. Earl Grey, a British peer, was Governor General of Canada in the first decade of the 20th century, and it was said he owned a ranch in the Kootenay Valley. Whether this property was near Grey's Creek is questionable, and I could establish no connection, but the spelling is suggestive.

For many years the general store on the lakeshore at Gray Creek was owned and operated by Arthur Lymbery, who made a lasting impression as a very determined individual. He said at one time that he came out from England in advance of a British peer who, for some reason, did not follow him. Lymbery battled the expropriation of land for roads on two occasions: first when the government built from his property south in the 1930s, and then when it went north with the new road construction in the 1940s. He did this staunchly and effectively, but the lakeside road, which detracted greatly from the property, went through anyway.

Throughout the 1930s, in the fine summer weather reputed to have been plentiful then, the hard-working farmers and fruit growers of the Kootenay Flats and the riverside benches, both near Creston, liked to spend weekends or, if they were better off than most, a week or two in cabins by the lovely beaches of Twin Bays, near Sanca. Later, the pleasant lakeside habitat was also enjoyed by Albertans, many from Calgary, who bought land and built cabins. It was a long day's drive from Calgary to the lake, but manageable in good weather. Two of these visitors turned out to be undertakers, and they found a good use for empty embalming fluid bottles, using them to build the walls of a cabin. This eventually became the Glass Castle, still a popular roadside tourist attraction.

It seems fitting to end this chapter with a mention of "Flying Phil," the Honourable Reverend P.A. Gaglardi, B.C.'s indomitable highways minister of the 1950s and 1960s. His first visit to the Creston area was in 1952, and it is still remembered by one of those who was there. After a very early morning arrival by plane at Cranbrook, and a substantial lunch in Creston, the minister fell asleep in his car on the smooth pavement between Creston and Wynndel.

He was suddenly rudely awakened when the car hit the numerous potholes on the road between Sirdar and Kuskanook. When he looked out the window at the rock faces on either side, which were not much farther apart than they had been when they were excavated in 1892 for a rail line, Gaglardi demanded to know why his driver had left the main road without his knowledge. It took some time to convince him that he was still on Highway 3. This section was always rough, mostly due to its being on a near-level grade. Railways do well with that, but roads do not.

Following this trip, Gaglardi arranged for some local logging operators to work on a road north from Kootenay Bay to Riondel, and this project dragged on over the next five years, from 1953 through 1957, with $50,000 spent to produce a low-standard road, seven miles in length. This was no bargain, but it was a better alternative than the first overland effort to access the east side of the lake. In 1892 an enterprising rancher from Toby Creek, near Invermere, drove a number of cattle through and over the Purcell Mountains, using Jumbo Pass and ending up at the northern end of Kootenay Lake. From there the beasts were shipped by boat to feed the miners at Riondel. A logging road now runs all the way up the east side of the lake from Riondel.

The rock faces viewed by the minister as he awoke near Kuskanook were moved back over time, but not by much. This unassuming but picturesque 49-mile stretch of roadway from the ferry to Creston never really warranted the classification of a main highway. It lacked any impressive structures such as large bridges or interchanges, or even any four-lane sections, and it was finally subjected to the indignity of having an "A" added to its number (becoming Highway 3A) when the Salmo-Creston cutoff opened in 1966 and ended its status as a trans-provincial highway.

Nonetheless, as the road link between Nelson, all the lakeside communities and Creston, and as one surrounded by magnificent mountains, it is still well used and enjoyed, and it has been a delightful part of British Columbia's history, as have the vessels that plied the lake in concert with, or in opposition to, it.

CHAPTER 3

The Crows Nest Railway

A railway built at the rate of 24 miles a month—a mile a day,
with the Lord's Day at rest.

In the last 13 years of the 19th century, an event took place in the southeast corner of British Columbia that gave one of the most energizing boosts to the economy of an area ever experienced anywhere. Quite simply, it was the discovery of minerals, which appeared to be there in huge amounts. While gold and copper were included marginally, the metals found in quantity were silver, lead and zinc. Copper was found west of the Kootenays in the Kettle River valley. A second underground payoff—less valued in small amounts, but treasured by the trainload— was coal.

The discoveries started in 1887, when a rich mineral find led to the creation of the Silver King Mine near Nelson. This was followed in 1890 by a similar discovery at Ainsworth, on the west shore of Kootenay Lake a few miles south of Kaslo. In 1891, more underground bounty was found on Red Mountain, near present-day Rossland, where the Le Roi Mine was established, and then again at a place called Sandon, 15 miles northwest of Kaslo, where the Payne Mine came into being, an operation that was to become the best dividend producer in B.C. for many years.

As if this were not enough, within the next two years huge deposits of ore were found a few miles farther east, near what is now the town of Kimberley, where two large mines, the North Star and the Sullivan,

These two CPR locomotives were all shined up to be photographed. They were wood burners, and the Crows Nest Railway opened up coal sources so they could be converted to burn that fuel. This reduced the embers in the air, which had caused huge grass fires on the prairies and forest fires in British Columbia.

sprang up, and a very rich mine called St. Eugene was created when ore was found at Moyie Lake—and these were only the major mining developments! Finally, in 1895, coal was found in great quantity in the area immediately west of Crowsnest Pass, near the present-day town of Fernie. Coal was also found just as liberally in Alberta on the other side of the pass.

Even the poor economy of North America in the early 1890s did not dampen the miners' and the promoters' enthusiasm for all of this, nor did the even more thrilling news of the Klondike late in the decade. Southern British Columbia was on its way, and the key to its economic success was transportation.

Unfortunately, the transportation situation was not good if you were a British Columbian hoping that the results of nature's beneficence would remain in Canada. The great transcontinental line put in by the Canadian Pacific Railway 10 years earlier ran far to the north, and the only way to move anything, other than by pack train, was to take it south into the United States. In that direction the Columbia and Kootenay rivers offered the cheapest means of transport—by tug and barge, mostly downstream—and when they were unavailable due to freezing conditions, there was the alternative of building railways alongside these rivers, and the Americans were putting these in just as fast as they could get charters from the Canadians to do so.

This railway intrusion started in 1889, when an American named D.C. Corbin opened a line that ran from Spokane to the foot of navigation on the Columbia River, a place called Little Dalles in Washington State near Trail. Corbin named his line the Spokane Falls and Northern Railway, and he immediately began negotiations to extend it north and east to Nelson in British Columbia. By 1893 Corbin's Nelson and Fort Sheppard Railway was running, connecting to the SF&N and terminating at a lakeshore point five miles outside Nelson city limits. (This out-of-town terminal was meant to placate the residents of Nelson, who opposed the Americans. The provincial government's only area of authority regarding an interprovincial railway at that time was inside city limits—elsewhere all was approved by Ottawa—so the premier, Theodore Davie, supported his citizens by refusing to let the Yankee railroaders into town.) Corbin also built a branch line from Northport, Washington, to Rossland. The ore from the Silver King Mine, and from many other mines within the Kootenay and Columbia watersheds, started flowing south.

But the transportation of B.C.'s riches southwards was not all done by Mr. Corbin and the SF&N. Another player got into the act, and he was a man worth some study. James Jerome Hill was a Canadian who was part owner of a railway in Minnesota and of riverboats on the Red River. He was an enthusiastic supporter of the CPR, and not just from nostalgia for his homeland. He had a personal motive because he ardently wished that part of the new railway would be located south of the border to assist his own operation and to avoid the Canadian

J.J. Hill, president of the Great Northern Railway, was a Canadian at heart as well as in nationality. Despite his animosity to the CPR board of directors and his desire to oppose them in the west, his foray into B.C. was part of his Canadianism. It was a difficult intervention in terms of profits and was largely dropped by his son upon Hill's death. All that remained of importance was the line from Everett, Washington, to Vancouver, which brought a rail bridge over the Fraser that was shared by other lines. Hill was generous to the citizens of Fernie, sending them $5,000 from his own account when the town was demolished by fire.

Precambrian Shield, a landscape of ancient rock most difficult to build anything in. He brought capital investment to the railway from New York State, and for that he became a director.

When the CPR's directors decided to keep the line entirely within Canada, Hill stormed out of the boardroom, taking all his capital with him, and he swore to harass and delay this new railway thereafter to the best of his ability. This was in 1883, and 10 years later he started a campaign against the CPR out west, which he enthusiastically pursued along the southern boundary of British Columbia for many years. In 1893, Hill's eastern American railway opened its western extension to Tacoma, Washington, becoming a transcontinental line. In the process it changed its name, becoming the Great Northern Railway. James J. Hill was its president, and one of its major targets in the west was to draw freight and passenger traffic away from the Canadian Pacific Railway.

The GN first leased boats and barges in Canada, then built them there. It moved people and goods (including ore from the Slocan region) south on Kootenay Lake from Kaslo, then up the Kootenay River (the Kootenai River in the United States) to Bonners Ferry, Idaho, which was a point on the GN main line. Hill then built a narrow-gauge railway from Nakusp to Kaslo by which he hauled ore from the Payne Mine and others in the Slocan area to Kootenay Lake.

Of course, a very interested observer of all this was William Cornelius Van Horne, the chief operating officer of the Canadian Pacific Railway, who was the face on the dragon in J.J. Hill's mind. In 1892, Van Horne's first move in the southern interior had been to build a rail line from Nelson to Robson, a distance of less than 20 miles, thus linking the Kootenay and Columbia river and lake transportation systems by the iron rail. His plan was to move ore from the Kootenay Lake mines by barge to Nelson and from there by rail to the Columbia, and then up that river and its lakes by tug and barge to the main CPR line at Revelstoke. The object was to handle all these natural riches in Canada and keep them away from the Americans. Unfortunately, the force of the Columbia's current and the ice on the lakes in winter made this operation difficult and grossly unprofitable, and they had to abandon it. Something else had to be done to thwart the Yankees.

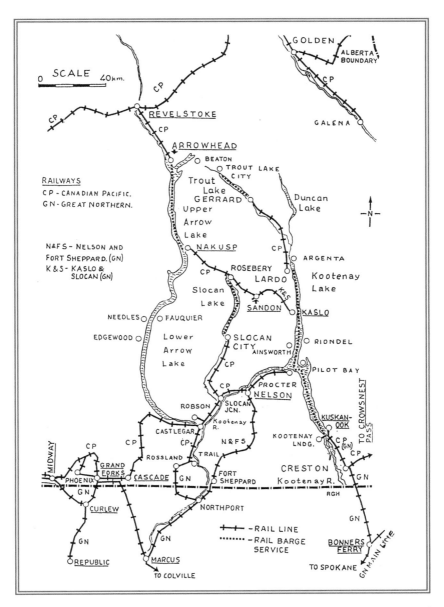

Railways of The West Kootenay: Shown here are the railways of the West Kootenay, Slocan and Arrow Lakes areas as they were in 1916, after the Great Northern Railway (GN) acquisitions were complete. The GN built the Kaslo & Slocan line in 1894 and 1895, and the CPR acquired it in 1912. D.C. Corbin built the Nelson and Fort Sheppard Railway in 1888 and a line from Northport to Rossland in 1896; the GN acquired all these in 1898. All other lines shown above are CPR.

As Van Horne learned more about Jim Hill's plans, he became even more apprehensive. One stunner was that Hill planned to build a spur line from a place called Rexford up to the Canadian border at a point where the Kootenay River enters the United States; from there he'd continue north and upstream to pick up the ore from the North Star Mine by rail. Rexford was a town in Montana on the GN main line and alongside the Kootenai River. It was located about 10 miles downstream of where the Kootenay entered the United States and was about 50 miles east of Bonners Ferry.

Another disturbing discovery was that Hill was planning to build another line farther east up to the Crowsnest Pass area to haul Canadian coal from there. (Hill later bought the Crow's Nest Pass Coal Company.) Less imminent, but just as threatening, was his intention to build a line from Bonners Ferry north to Kootenay Lake. This would replace the onerous upstream tug and barge haul to Bonners Ferry with a riverside railway. Jim Hill did in fact build all these lines, and he built them in the 1890s.

Van Horne's retaliation came late in 1897 when the CPR started building a line from Lethbridge, Alberta, into B.C. and on to Kuskanook, a small landing at the south end of Kootenay Lake. This was part of a charter proposal for a railway from Crowsnest Pass to the coast which in 1890 had been granted to a prominent early settler, Colonel J. Baker, who was the MLA for the East Kootenay and later became a B.C. cabinet minister.[1] He sold his charter to the CPR in 1896. (Baker did not proceed with construction because he was not able to procure funding from August Heinze, the American magnate who built the smelter at Trail and the rail line from Trail to Rossland.)

This proposal involved two of B.C.'s major belts of mountains: first a full crossing of the Rocky Mountains, half of which were in Alberta, and then a climb through the first range of the Columbia Mountains, the Purcell Range, within B.C. In the 1880s the CPR had built a line south from Calgary to Fort Macleod,[2] but it did not continue on from Fort Macleod to Lethbridge because of the coulee of the Oldman River, a gash in the prairie over a mile wide and 300 feet deep. When the decision was made to go west from Fort Macleod, the CPR added construction east from Fort Macleod to Lethbridge. The estimated total distance to be covered was 330 miles.

The CPR also intended to continue the line up the west side of Kootenay Lake to Procter, along the south shore of the West Arm of Kootenay Lake to Nelson and, eventually, farther west. The West Arm section was built in good time, but the line along the main lake to Procter did not happen right away (see chapter 2).

To handle the great cost of these proposals, the CPR decided to visit the Dominion government, not totally as a supplicant, as most railway builders in Canada did then, but also as a bargainer. The bargain that was agreed to in this case became known as the Crows Nest Pass Agreement, and it was concluded in September 1897. It had repercussions far beyond the building of this line and became one of the most controversial railway agreements in Canada's history. In short, it involved a government subsidy of $11,000 for each of the 330 miles from Lethbridge to Kuskanook, to a total of $3.63 million, in exchange for the CPR's promise to reduce rates on grain shipped to Thunder Bay and to cede to the government 50,000 acres of coal land in the Crowsnest area. The agreement implied that the CPR would maintain the new rates for grain shipments in perpetuity, thus infuriating all other shippers in western Canada who were not so favoured. The subsidy came through.[3]

Before this happened, but as soon as it was sure of the money, the CPR started work on the eastern end of the railway in July 1897. At first the directors balked at bridging across the main gorge of the Oldman. Instead they had the main line bypass Lethbridge, ran a spur line in to that community, and trestled only across the Oldman's south fork. The railway put up with this arrangement, including steeper grades, for only 12 years before replacing it with a trestle bridge right across the gorge in 1909. The Oldman railway trestle is one of the largest in Canada, at 5,328 feet long and 314 feet high.

When work was suspended in the winter of 1897, the crews had laid track to a point 12 miles east of the pass. In their hurry to rush supplies and equipment through, most of the initial track laying was on bare ground, so it is likely that proper ballasting still had to be done. But the stage was set for crews to commence work at the earliest date in the new year when winter's grasp was broken at that 4,400-foot elevation, and then they would be on their 194-mile way up to the pass and on to Kootenay Lake.

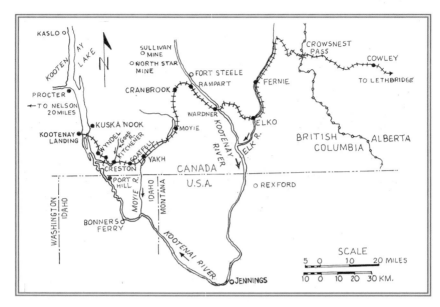

The Crows Nest Railway: This line was built in record time in 1898.

Assuming that they could not start work in the field before March at the earliest, for them to build rail grade and lay track for 194 miles between March and October, a period of eight months, was an achievement almost beyond belief. The credit for it goes primarily to one man, Michael J. Haney, otherwise known as Big Mike or the Irish Prince. This was the same man who bulldozed the railway east through the Fraser Canyon and beyond for Andrew Onderdonk, the contractor for the CPR main line in the 1880s. After that Haney plied his trade farther east until W.C. Van Horne grabbed him for the Crowsnest Pass work, which was to be the fastest of them all.

They did a lot of preparatory work before March. Headquarters for the operation was Fort Macleod, and it was there that Haney organized the prefabrication of timber bridge and trestle parts, his specialty and a strong point of his Fraser Canyon work. Their first move when spring came was to put through a tote road for the 70 miles from Crowsnest Pass to Wardner, a port on the upper Kootenay River. The road was probably located on a cleared trail left along their line by the surveyors.

West of Wardner there were already trails in existence, including the Dewdney Trail (which ran west from what is now Cranbrook), and the railway crews widened them to take wagons and cattle when useful to them. Soon there was a stagecoach running on part of this network. Wardner was also served by river craft from Jennings, Montana.

On the other side of the Purcells lay Creston, which was also on the Kootenay River after it had returned to British Columbia from its loop southwards. Creston was then called Fisher, and it was supplied by vessels plying the Kootenay northwards from Bonners Ferry, Idaho. In addition, supplies were carried in via the Summit Creek Trail over the mountains from Salmo.

There were more ancient trails in the area, the premier one being the old Walla Walla Trail from lower down on the Columbia, up through Spokane and Bonners Ferry to the Moyie River, and up that stream to the upper Kootenay. (David Thompson travelled this last part, from Bonners Ferry, on one of his trips.) It was an international connection that was much used when gold was found on Wild Horse Creek in 1863.

To complete 194 miles in eight months, the CPR crews obviously could not start at one end and progressively lay track; that would have required them to produce 24 miles a month from one work site. The answer was multiple operations, each with its own camp. The camps were spread out along the way, assigned an achievable mileage, and leapfrogged other camps as the work progressed. This was why they built the tote road first.

Haney did not hesitate. He immediately brought in 5,000 men and 2,000 teams of horses for the job. With 2,000 men for general work and bridges, this would leave 3,000 men for grade building and track laying, spread out in multiple crews along the way with, say, 150 men and 50 teams per camp. This is speculation, of course, but it is supported in part by recollections gathered from men who worked on the line, retired in Creston and were interviewed in the 1940s and 1950s.[4]

The logistics were formidable. How do you feed so many men and horses, taking into consideration the conditions they faced? A man by the name of Clem Payette gives some of the answers. He says cattle were assembled at Cowley, a small Alberta settlement 30 miles east of Crowsnest, from where teams of five cowboys drove up to 60 steers at a time over the 100 miles of rough trail through to Wardner. Several herds left each week, providing fresh meat to each camp every two or three days. There was no cold storage, so they ate it right away, and the railway work crews consumed up to 300 beeves per month. They also baked bread in field ovens. Payette says their food was of the plainest sort.

Ernest Hoskins, another retiree at Creston, who left the North West Mounted Police to work on the railway early in 1898, tells us that he drove a four-horse wagon to Wardner and back continually throughout that season, along with others doing the same thing. They delivered oats and hay for the horses, powder for blasting, camp supplies, you name it, several times a week. They also picked up supplies at Wardner and carried them forward, and of course they were accompanied by horse teams hauling in bridge parts, and rails and ties. Track was laid as soon as possible, with the ties on bare ground. They used the unfinished track to start up a work-train supply service from the east and to bring in steam shovels and pile drivers, about the only mechanical equipment that they had. Other than this, the railway was described by many of these old-timers as a creation of manpower and horsepower.

Before going further into their equipment and methods, it is necessary to describe the challenge they faced. They were building through the Rocky Mountains, albeit over a generally unconstricted pass and one of the lowest at 4,450 feet above sea level (Pine Pass and Yellowhead Pass are lower). Their route then descended the western slope of the Rockies for 30 miles by way of the Elk River valley, a steep mountain river valley that was very rocky in places, with one canyon, and they finally bridged that river. After that they crossed the Rocky Mountain Trench, here consisting of the wide valley of the Upper Kootenay, bridging the river channel in the course of their work.

The Purcell Range followed. At this latitude it consisted of much gentler and lower mountains than occurred farther north. Here they went through a low pass called Goatfell, which led to the Goat River valley. They bridged the Goat at Kitchener and went on from there to the Kootenay valley and lake.

In addition to a lot of hard rock in the Elk River valley, and rock work encountered intermittently from there on, they had to cope with difficult clay and silt subsoils stretching for miles on either side of Cranbrook.

When it was wet, these materials led to the notorious gumbo slides experienced on the project, which injured, and at times buried, the men working below the cut slopes. It was all heavily timbered virgin country, with heavy rock cuttings in some sections requiring several tunnels, and numerous bridges and trestles.

To describe their work practices, no better account can be found than that of Henry Raglin, who retired to Creston after 41 years of railway work. He tells of one camp where an army of 150 men attacked the project every day with short-handled shovels, loading long trains with gravel at a wage of a dollar per day. There would be large numbers of hard-sweating men and horses with slush scrapers, wheel scrapers and fresnos (a rolling drum scraper that both scraped and then carried the soil, named after the place it was first made). They also let small contracts to excavate and move dirt by hand-shovel and wheelbarrow.

Another experienced railwayman, James Compton, who worked on bridges, says that when they reached Wardner in August 1898, the men worked up to their waists in water to rush the steel bridge spans across as soon as the water level started dropping. Steel arrived in Fernie in July.

The accident rate was far from acceptable compared to modern standards. Twenty-three men were killed when a bridge collapsed in a sudden vicious windstorm near Lethbridge, and three men died when they were blown off a structure in Crowsnest Pass. Other mishaps occurred because they worked very long hours, sometimes days through, only stopping for meals.

Their work on rock was extremely primitive in comparison to today's methods—all rock drilling was done by hand. In the pass the wind often blew so hard that drilling could not be done because they could not risk an unbalanced mis-stroke by the man wielding the sledgehammer. The men on these rock operations were almost all from Sweden, brought out by the immigration program of the time. The East Kootenay population reflects that to this day.

The method of making the men's temporary camps was interesting. They generally scorned tents, preferring temporary log buildings with wood-shake roofing and siding. Compton was critical of the sanitary arrangements in these camps, saying that there were more railway workers in the temporary hospital at the Goat River crossing (now Kitchener) and the fine St. Eugene Hospital at Cranbrook suffering from disease than from accidents. He says the hospital at Goat River lacked one thing—nurses. At St. Eugene the very competent and well-known Dr. R.F. Green did his best, but typhoid was rampant, along with other maladies.

Here something must be said that is uncomplimentary to Haney. He drove his men too hard, housed them too poorly and paid them too little. Unlike the men involved in Fraser Canyon work during the 1880s, the majority of the labourers were not Chinese. The Crows Nest Railway was built in the midst of the Canadian government's huge immigration drive under Interior Minister Clifford Sifton. Asians were not included in this, and the majority of the immigrants who worked on the railway came from eastern Europe, Scandinavia and Britain.

Eventually the outcry forced Sifton to carry out an investigation of the treatment of labourers on this work. His report was extremely critical, citing poor accommodation, bad sanitary conditions and poor wages. The CPR was actually paying lower wages than Andrew Onderdonk had paid 15 years earlier, as low as a dollar a day, and never more than $1.75. Bridge workers got $2.75 a day. There is no evidence that anything was done in response to Sifton's report. Perhaps the project was finished before the government could grind into action.

When the railway came into the Fort Steele area there was an intriguing series of negotiations to acquire land for the major railway depot planned there. A man called John Galbraith and his wife had arrived in the region in 1869, and John's brother Robert came in 1870. Fort Steele is located where Wild Horse Creek joins the Kootenay River, and to serve the Wild Horse gold rush, the Galbraiths started a ferry service across the Kootenay River. The settlement that came into being was soon called Galbraiths' Ferry, and Robert Galbraith finally owned most of Fort Steele, the town that succeeded it. He also pre-empted most of Joseph's Prairie, a prime area of flat land across the river.

The CPR liked the look of Joseph's Prairie, but it was willing to locate at Fort Steele—provided it received the free handout of land it always demanded of a town or settlement favoured with its presence. Galbraith wanted the CPR in Fort Steele but demanded payment for the land, and he would not consider giving up anything at Joseph's Prairie. Both parties dug in their heels to wait the other out. Robert Galbraith finally succumbed to an offer for Joseph's Prairie from Colonel J. Baker, who promptly gave half of it to the CPR, set up a general store and prospered, as the CPR built its divisional point at what became the city of Cranbrook. Fort Steele died on the vine.

So there they were, the job complete and one year left until the end of the century. In all the old-timers' stories they talk of ending the line at Kuskanook, but the CPR did not finally end its grand project there. A few miles south of Kuskanook the construction was extended across the partially submerged area south of the lake to a point on the west side suitable for a landing, which was named Kootenay Landing. This involved four and a quarter miles of trestle and a swing bridge over the main channel. And in 1899 the CPR built two spur lines, one to the North Star Mine and one to Fort Steele. These were completed by "what few of us were left," according to Jim Compton.

The name for the railway has varied. The first charter in B.C., granted to Colonel Baker, was for The Crow's Nest and Kootenay Lake Railway. When Baker gave this charter to the CPR, the name had become The British Columbia Southern Line, and the CPR used that name but also referred to it as the Crow's Nest Pass line. As Crows Nest Railway was the name used by the men working on the job, it is our title here.

The place names on the map of the railway also merit a look. Most were nonexistent before the railway came. Wardner was there, but only just. It was named after James F. Wardner, a mining promoter from the United States, who was one of the first to ship ore down the Kootenay River. Wardner founded a number of towns named after him. Wardner, Idaho, is one. Cranbrook was named by Colonel Baker after the town in Kent, England, where he was born. Creston was named after a town in the U.S. Its original name, Fisher, honoured Jack Fisher, who discovered Wild Horse Creek's gold. Fernie was named after William Fernie, a foreman on the crew that built the Dewdney Trail. He found most of the coal around the town named after him. Fort Steele, a name that preceded the railway, was named after Colonel Sam Steele of the NWMP.

Kuskanook and Yahk were Native names, and they were there before the railway. Port Hill, later changed to Porthill, was named after a prospector called Chippy Hill, who sparked a very temporary gold rush at Sanca, a few miles up the lakeshore from Kuskanook. Port Hill was originally called Okinook, and it was the site of a North West Company and later an HBC fort, which was abandoned long before the 1890s. Procter was the name of a real estate agent from Nelson.

Although there was still much work to be done, including completing the makeshift bridges, which they called "skeleton structures," M.J. Haney was not around after 1898. After the rails were laid to Kuskanook, when winter turned to spring in 1899, the name, if not the man, seems to have disappeared. Nothing further is heard of Michael J. Haney. But it is reported that, in March 1899, a man calling himself Michael J. Heney came up to the Klondike, where the gold rush was in full swing. He walked from Skagway over the White Pass route through the mountains, and then returned to Skagway.

One version of what happened next states that, purely by chance, he overheard two men talking in a restaurant. The two were from England and represented Close Brothers, a financing firm, and they were evidently considering the possibility of building a railway over White Pass and on to Whitehorse, which they said was quite impossible. Michael Heney spoke to them and convinced them that it was possible, and they agreed to give him a contract to provide the labour for the job. He started out with a contract for labour and ended up as the contractor of record for the White Pass and Yukon Railway. He had four of the most difficult coastal miles done in four months, and the 103 miles to Whitehorse were completed by July 29, 1900. The railway's official history confirms that the name on the contract was Heney.

After promoting the Klondike Mines Railway, with local lines near Dawson City, Michael Heney went on to build the Copper River and North west Railway in Alaska, now extended to become the rail line from Valdez to Fairbanks. It was reputed to be the most difficult of them all. Is it the same man? It has to be. Why the change of name? Who knows?

It is unfortunate that Michael J. Haney did not achieve the great credit the Crows Nest Railway project should have brought him. Certainly it did not have the national importance of the Fraser Canyon line, but for ramming through 194 miles of track in eight months it need take no second place. And what other railway work had 60 cattle driven 100 miles through the length of the work two and three times a week, and had a total workforce that ate up 300 steers a month?

Postscript

In May 1948, this author was posted by the B.C. Department of Public Works to a crew supervising road construction on the southern trans-provincial highway running east from Wardner, B.C. With the contracting company there were several rock drillers and blasters who were veterans from the Crows Nest Railway construction. Emigrating from Scandinavia to this work in their early 20s, they were still hard at it in their early 70s, 50 years later—they did not believe in retirement.

These were the ones who stayed with it, differing from the great majority of that force of 5,000 men who went on to other things, mainly farming on the prairies or in the East Kootenay, and raising families in the process. These hard-rock men were single and they were characters, men you meet and do not forget, and at that late date their English was still not that good. (One incident remains in this author's memory, when one of them seriously hurt another in a fist fight. It came about when one left his canvas water bag on a stump which the other blasted.) And what changes they saw! Horses and fresnos replaced by huge diesel-driven motor scrapers, and compressed air driving steel bits into rock 10 times as fast and 10 times as far as hand work.

Their most entertaining tale was of the difficulty of getting enough to eat on that long train trip out from Montreal to Calgary. Not only could they not read the menus, they also could not converse with the stewards, and in any case they had little money. They simply pointed to the first and cheapest item on the menu, and thus got orange juice for breakfast and soup for lunch and dinner. The Hon. Clifford Sifton's immigration program put them on the train, and apparently that was it.

Even if they spent a working lifetime on the prairie, these men and women remembered the East Kootenay area and the lovely mountain views and the climate—one that lacked the searing summers and the driving blizzards of the flat lands. In retirement, many returned to the Creston valley. After all, if they wanted to go back to the prairies and visit, or maybe bring their friends over, it was only an overnight train trip.

CHAPTER 4

WEATHER AND ROADS IN BRITISH COLUMBIA

Nature often surprises when mountains and B.C. weather are concerned.

The effects of bad weather on B.C.'s roads are as varied as its climate zones. The province's mountainous terrain, intricate river networks and often unpredictable temperature fluctuations create ongoing challenges that arise from weather at its worst: avalanches, debris torrents, ice jams, and snow and ice on the roads.

Avalanches

Probably the first thing that comes to mind when one thinks of weather and roads in the mountains is avalanches. They certainly have the most spectacular effect on roads, are the most difficult events to predict and often cause the longest road closures. It is also difficult to decide when the danger is over. British Columbia has many mountains that are subject to heavy winter snowfall, and temperature changes and gravity regularly combine to send the snow roaring down the mountainsides. There is visual proof of this for all to see in the form of avalanche paths—strips on the sides of the mountains that have been swept bare of trees, show white with snow in winter and are kept that way year after year.

There is a wide range in climate between British Columbia's coastal areas and its Interior plateaus. For example, Hope receives an average of 1.52 metres of precipitation yearly, and Merritt only 0.3 metres (all

This shows the avalanche paths or tracks in the Boston Bar Creek valley, which were first described by a Royal Engineers sapper in 1849 while he was blazing a trail from Fort Hope to Boston Bar. He described them as "signs of fearsome snow falls"—and the engineers went elsewhere.

water equivalent). Within a distance of 21 miles in the Coldwater River valley, the precipitation varies from 16 inches yearly down to 4 inches. All this, of course, affects the type of snow movement that occurs. The public has come to think that the term "avalanche" only applies to huge thundering events that wipe out villages, but the word is used for all snow movements caused by the force of gravity, no matter how extensive (or minor) the movement may be.

Factors in the variation of avalanche type are the depth and stratification of the snow, and the dimensions of the initial break in the snow cover. Depending on the condition that the snow was in when it broke away, there can be a loose snow avalanche or a slab avalanche, a surface avalanche or a full-depth avalanche (the latter two terms describe whether it is just the surface layer or all the snow that is moving). According to the humidity of the snow there can be a dry-snow or a wet-snow avalanche; the nature of the terrain can produce an unconfined avalanche or a channelled avalanche; the form of movement can be an airborne powder avalanche or a flowing avalanche.

The results of each type are, of course, very different. A high-velocity airborne powder avalanche usually generates a highly destructive wind

Seen here are two slopes with moving avalanches. At left is a dry avalanche; at right is a wet one.

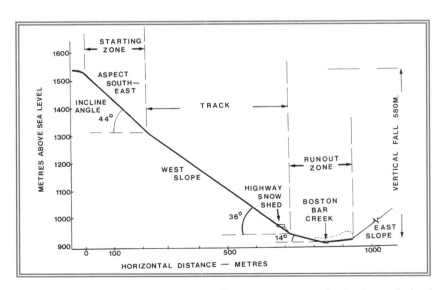

Profile of an Avalanche Path: This is a diagram of the Great Bear No. 5 avalanche slope at the head of Boston Bar Creek valley. Its runout zone is shared by Rhodes No. 5 from across the valley, and the two together are twice the trouble. (To convert from metres to feet, multiply by 3.28.)

blast, whereas a channelled wet-snow avalanche on a relatively flat slope can move very slowly and not create any noticeable air movement at all.

Avalanches follow a standard path. First, there is the start or starting zone, where the unstable snow first breaks away and starts to move. The starting zone aspect refers to the direction in which it faces. Then there is the vertical fall, which is the vertical distance between start and stop, the latter area being the runout zone. Finally there is the incline, which is the slope angle of the path of the avalanche. This is usually measured for each of the three portions of that path—the start zone, the track and the runout zone.

The goal of highway designers in avalanche areas is to keep the road away from all potential avalanche paths, but it is difficult to avoid encroaching on runout zones when building roads in narrow mountain valleys. When two avalanche paths from either side of a valley coincide in a common runout zone, the task is impossible. In one part of the Boston Bar Creek valley, through which the Coquihalla Highway runs, the problem was solved by a snow shed.

Several major B.C. highways are in the paths of potential avalanches: Highway 1, the Trans-Canada, is at risk for about 30 miles in the Eagle and Rogers Pass areas; Highway 5, the Coquihalla, 14 miles in the Coquihalla Pass area; Highway 3, 12 miles between Hope and Princeton, and another 6 miles in the Salmo-Creston section. Other routes with smaller areas or less intensity of threat are Highway 97 in the Pine Pass area; Highway 99, Britannia to Pemberton area; Highway 16, the Terrace to Prince Rupert area and the Mount Robson area; Highway 1 through the Fraser Canyon.

The first line of defence against the avalanche hazard is to close the highway when the risk is high. The average length of closures for each of the highways mentioned above depends on various factors. Rogers Pass, for example, has an average closure of only 4 hours, due mainly to its seven snow sheds. The Coquihalla Highway has one shed and two aerial tramways and probably a similar average closure. In comparison, the Salmo-Creston section of Highway 3 has an average closure of 14 hours during years of heavy snowfall. Although short in terms of the length of highway affected, this section has no snow sheds and, more importantly, receives an unpredictable annual snowfall, which on one occasion reached as high as 50 feet.

Measuring the snowfall on the Coquihalla summit: The recorder in the upper photo is for measuring the intensity and direction of the snowfall. In this view, the snow around it is 15 feet deep. The three towers in the photo below it are, from the left: a precipitation gauge, which is linked to a circular snow pillow at its base; a temperature and humidity recorder; and finally, the same recorder shown in the upper photo. This measurement of snow started in the early 1970s.

Below, this helicopter is on its belly in deep snow while the pilot has gone to change the charts on the snow-measuring instruments at the Coquihalla summit weather station. He has to be quick or his craft will freeze in, and he probably has to wear snowshoes.

Avalanches affect other modes of transportation and other activities, and are fatal to various degrees. The most costly in lives so far is one that occurred in Rogers Pass during the early years of the CPR transcontinental railway, which took the lives of 58 men in March 1910. It was followed in number of fatalities by a rock and snow slide at Britannia Beach in March 1915, which took the lives of 57 men, women and children. Since then, lives lost on railways or highways in avalanches or snow slides have been measured in much lower numbers; two highway workers on skis, watching for evidence of snow buildup north of Stewart, were killed by that which they sought in January 1999.

Avalanche pileup and movement of ice and snow can have other longer-lasting effects. A road to a mine in the Slocan area of British Columbia was filled to a depth of 170 feet by a snow slide in the 1890s. It took six years to melt, and the mine management had to construct a tunnel through it to get the miners to work. In February 1965, at the Granduc Mine near Stewart, a mine built on the moraine of a glacier of the same name, an avalanche blocked the adit portal to the mine— 68 men were put in danger, and 26 of them died of suffocation. At its summit, the road to Granduc has been subjected to as much as 100 feet of snowfall in one season.

Another measure used to downgrade avalanche hazards is to move snow to a diversion ditch or containment area, but to clear the roadway of the amount of snow that fell at Granduc requires a steep sidehill leading down from the roadside. Fortunately there were two such valleys to provide this. At the summit between them, however, with no sidehill, the only option was to drive a tunnel, which had to be constantly heated in winter. Otherwise it would have filled with icicles.

This tunnel was 8,900 feet in length and sparse in overburden—in other words, there was relatively little depth of ground above it, which made a long tunnel much easier to build because air vents could be readily installed. It was therefore well ventilated in addition to being well lit. It was also a haven of safety for the snowplowing crews when nature did its worst. Access to the mine in winter was primarily by ski-equipped planes or helicopters, but if the 26-mile road had been left unplowed, the 20 to 30 feet of snow pack on the ground would have caused too much damage when it melted.

Besides closing the road, the only foolproof protection from avalanches is snow sheds, but they are expensive. The one on the Coquihalla Highway for the Great Bear avalanche path, for example, cost $15 million.

Another option is to offset the danger before it builds up. This is done by watching the snow accumulate and by triggering smaller, controlled movements of the snow from time to time, usually by using explosive charges that are either thrown from a gun or an avalauncher, or delivered by an aerial tramway. The use of aerial tramways is limited to areas where several paths are close together, such as in Boston Bar Creek valley on the Coquihalla Highway, where there are two of them.

The use of aerial tramways, or ropeways, has been ingeniously pursued in Europe, where they use up to 10 quite large explosive charges in one set. These can be placed along the ropeway at carefully planned locations and are lowered by remote radio and computer control. Each charge has a metal bell-shaped cover over it to protect the rope, which is at least 33 yards above it. The charges are set off together, and the system works in any kind of weather or conditions.

Top: Seen here are the Great Bear avalanche slopes at the head of Boston Bar Creek valley, beside the Coquihalla Highway. It cost B.C. taxpayers $15 million for a snow shed plus a few million more for diversion trenches and containment basins to render these slopes safe.

Bottom: The Great Bear Snow Shed, at the summit of the Coquihalla, is 27 miles east of Hope. It is 306 yards long and has six lanes. Built within 10 months in 1985 and 1986, it is lighted inside, and the transition pavement at the entrances is heated to prevent icing in winter. The shed roof and walls can withstand a high-speed impact of a 40-foot-depth of snow and debris.

These photographs show various types of avalauncher. Two are mounted on trailers (top left and bottom); the one at top right is in a permanent tower and shows the projectiles used. They are 14 inches long, 3 inches in diameter, have fins for straight flight and are primed in flight by air pressure to explode on contact with the snow. The range is 3,000 yards, and the misfire rate is low. These projectiles are biodegradable, in contrast to an army howitzer shell, which remains a hazard if it misfires (some have been found in highway ditches). Avalaunchers may be fired from a truck bed or from a trailer, but they are more effective if mounted in a permanent tower, with firing courses established in advance for use in zero visibility.

Debris Torrents

In the early 1980s, a series of debris torrents wreaked havoc on Highway 99 and its creek crossings between Horseshoe Bay and Britannia Beach in the Lower Mainland. The first was in late October 1981, when a bridge over Magnesia Creek was destroyed by a massive debris torrent and slide. Nine late-night travellers died.

On February 11, 1983, it happened again at Alberta Creek, and two teenagers were killed by the flood while sleeping in a trailer nearby. In November 1983, no lives were lost when Charles Creek bridge, two

private bridges and a BC Railway bridge were swept away, and in 1984 there were some minor slides with no bridges lost. This improvement was in part due to intensive winter patrols at night and also to the continuing construction of debris catchment facilities where the highway crossed creeks subject to this hazard.

There is little doubt that Japan has more debris torrents than anywhere else in the world. That country has not been idle in combatting them, and Japanese advice was sought by the B.C. highways department. This was provided generously, and the information was most useful in the design of protection works. Especially interesting was a movie taken of a debris torrent in full fury, which was loaned by the Japanese highway authority to its B.C. counterpart.[1]

As well as repairing the damage and constructing protective culverts, the highways department took immediate action to provide better

The drawing at the top shows one type of culvert inlet protection against debris torrents. The bottom photo shows an alternative protection. An area in the creek course upstream of the bridge is levelled so debris will be dumped there. Then the creek channel under the bridge is concreted so that any remaining debris carried this far will be shed here.

warnings for travellers, setting up five weather stations at various elevations, and also installing numerous telephone stations along the roadway for the public to use. A department report in 1984 identified seven debris-torrent danger areas along the road as the major problem, with the investigation continuing.

Debris torrents occur when a thin mantle of soil and humus on an exceedingly steep rock slope becomes totally saturated by continuous heavy rain. This sodden material sometimes suddenly breaks loose from the rock below it and slides away, first into folds of the land such as creek valleys, and then down these valleys. It accelerates due to the steepness of the slope, and it constantly picks up more soil and debris until it finally reaches its conclusion when the slope runs out.

The urgency of the situation in 1981 demanded an immediate and close examination of all the ravine slopes on that section of the highway to detect the imminence of further slides. The highways department decided to do this by helicopter, but some of the creek valleys were so narrow and steep-sided that they presented a problem, primarily because the helicopter could not turn around in such close confines when it was flying so low.

One pilot proposed a method to overcome the problem. He flew up the ravine for the distance necessary, then sideslipped the machine backward and down out of the gorge before moving over to the next valley in quick order, all the time coping with intermittent cloudiness. For this writer, who was a passenger on some of these trips, this did the job well, but the procedure was one that was not easy to forget. (Sad to say, this pilot died a few months later when he crashed while flying unaccompanied.) All such ravines were inspected by this and more conventional flying methods, and several potential slide sites were noted. More important was the discovery of an ancient log dam used in very early logging, which posed a threat if it collapsed. This was rectified.

The only good feature of debris torrents is that when they happen, a large amount of the more vulnerable overburden is removed. As a result, and because there have not been heavy, continuous rainstorms of the intensity or frequency experienced in the early 1980s, debris torrents have been less of a hazard on this road in recent years.

Debris torrents are experienced infrequently in similar weather conditions on other highways bounded by mountains in B.C., but never to the extent seen on Highway 99 in the early 1980s. These quirks of nature have been observed propelling a wave of large boulders and other debris to a height of over 20 feet and at speeds of up to 30 miles per hour. This can result in "one-time" debris depositions of up to 326,988 cubic yards.

Those on Highway 99 were of much smaller volume, but one area known to have such large debris movements is west of Floods in the Fraser Valley. The mountains involved there are the Skagit Range of the Cascade Mountains, which are higher than those at Howe Sound, and the mantle of overburden is much thicker—3 to 10 feet deep. Saturation to the extent required to bare the rock is much less common and usually involves snow melt as well as heavy continuous rain, but it does happen. When it does, the momentum of the torrent when it reaches the foot of the mountains and enters the alluvial plain of the Fraser can carry the flood water and debris for thousands of feet. Often the outmost part of it ends up across the Trans-Canada Highway.

Travellers using that highway often wonder where the debris they see being removed came from. They find it hard to believe that it came from the mountains half a mile away, but nature often surprises when mountains and B.C. weather are concerned.

Rainfall, Roads and Glaciers

Glaciers do not like rain, and they especially do not like it in October. That is the month when they reach their weakest state after prolonged exposure to summer sun and fall rains, and they await the snows of winter to restore them. This can be a problem when roads and glaciers meet.

The road from Stewart to Cassiar probably has the greatest number of nearby glaciers in British Columbia, particularly the section in the Bear River valley from Stewart to Bear Pass and on to Meziadin Lake junction. Bear Pass is the termination of a glacier, and Glacier Creek, which is a few miles out of town and flows under a road bridge into Bear River, drains four glaciers, including the Bear River Glacier.

By 1961, that glacier was in full retreat and only partially filled the pass. (This was in contrast to the situation in 1898, when it blocked the pass and frustrated Premier John Herbert Turner's plans to build a railway from Stewart to Teslin. It cost him an election later in the year.) The rough road that skirted around the toe of the glacier, climbing up and down in an arc across the rocky slope of the other side of the gorge, was being built into a highway that year. The toe that road skirted held back a small lake, Strohn Lake, with a small iceberg in it. Such lakes are scientifically known as kettle lakes.

On October 6, 1961, 11 inches of rainfall fell on the Stewart area in 24 hours. That rain fell as snow above the 3,000-foot level. One week later, on October 13, more than 12 inches of rain fell in a similar period, but by then the temperature had risen to 70°F, and that mild air lay all over the mountains.

Disaster came on the night immediately after the second rainfall, when no one was on the road up the Bear River valley. The rain filled Strohn Lake to overflowing, and it washed over the quickly weakening glacier tongue. The pressure of this water broke a 40-foot-wide hole in the tongue. The lake drained out as a toilet tank would empty when the plug was pulled. (Maybe this is why they were named kettle lakes, because they are poured out from time to time.) The resultant torrent of

By 1961 the Bear River Glacier, viewed here from Bear Pass, was in full retreat.

water, mud and rocks surged down the Bear River valley and washed out the roadway and the overburden down to bedrock for miles. Anyone on the road at that time would not have survived. (This same kettle lake was created five times between 1958 and 1962, and each October the water drained out and caused havoc all the way down the Bear River valley.[2] Its yearly disappearing act was put to an end in 1963, when the highways department dug a channel through the toe of the glacier to drain the lake before its yearly buildup. This was done by bulldozers equipped with special ice grippers on the tracks.)

A few miles outside Stewart at Bitter Creek, another creek draining glaciers, an 80-foot-long log stringer bridge was carried 2,000 feet downstream and demolished by a huge outburst of storm water. The creek channel split into four lesser waterways, and four temporary bridges were required to restore the road. They were placed up to 500 feet downstream of the original site of the bridge. One of these temporary spans was subsequently washed out, and all were eventually replaced by a new bridge at the original site.

Events at Glacier Creek were even more traumatic and, in many of the road workers' experience, unprecedented. At least one of the glaciers at the head of Glacier Creek must have had a kettle lake in place, and maybe all four of them had one. That lake (or those lakes), overflowing with all the water from the tumultuous rainfall, may have broken a hole in the tongue of the glacier, or floated up the mass of ice (which is another thing that happens to glaciers in flood conditions), and immediately spilled out through or beneath it.

As glaciers advance, they scrape soil and debris ahead of them, then drop it behind them as they recede. This is called glacial till, and when the lake gushed out down Glacier Creek, most of the glacial till went with it. Water, glacial till and all kinds of debris that was picked up along the way arrived at the foot of the mountains and spread out into a fan on the level ground. The fan was a few hundred feet wide at the top, 2,000 feet wide at its outer edge and 2,000 feet long. Its total volume was estimated to be well over a quarter million cubic yards. The debris filled up and completely obliterated the creek bed, and the creek picked up and partially buried the timber bridge's-60-foot-span before leaving it.

This happened at night, and the next morning the road crews found a slightly bedraggled-looking bridge without a creek. It was partially buried and its abutments had disappeared.

When the regional highway engineer inspected the situation later that day, the creek, which had returned to a more normal volume of flow by then, was meandering around the fan, trying to decide on a permanent location. It eventually settled on one well removed from the original channel. Watching this, one got an eerie feeling that this was how all landscape was created and how all creek channels and valleys had been formed from the beginning of time—nothing in nature is really permanent.

After a new set of abutments had been built, bulldozers straightened the new channel and skidded the faithful old structure over to its new position on the newly relocated road. Thus the roadway was restored across the fan and on up to the pass, and all was as before. Just one more battle of roads versus weather.[3]

When nature lay down the fan, it followed the laws of physics, grading the material by weight in distance carried. In other words, the creek dropped the heaviest rocks first, and at the bottom edge of the fan there was simply a black sludge. The bridge, by good fortune, was originally located near the foot of the fan; if it had been elsewhere, it would never have remained relatively intact. Within a decade the lower half of the fan was covered with vegetation and appeared little different from its surroundings. By the 1980s, when the main road from Stewart to Watson Lake was completed, the Bear River Glacier had retreated right out of the pass. Drivers moving quickly on the new road were puzzled to see a rough gravel roadway built up the face of the rocky hillside and back down again, but although the glacier was gone, the road workers did not forget the night of the rains.

Ice Jams

In British Columbia, ice forms to greatly different thicknesses on the Interior rivers from year to year. As well, the thickness of ice cover on one river can vary from place to place, due mainly to the unpredictable temperature fluctuations experienced during B.C. winters.

The way this river ice breaks up in the spring is also unpredictable, and often surprising. In the northern part of the province, ice on large rivers can break up and move out in a few days, or the breakup can take weeks. On remote rivers in the north, large ice jams occur regularly, unobserved and with no one being the wiser. In any part of the Interior of the province, ice can increase in volume incrementally and then move, either slowly or quickly, in small or massive amounts, or else it can rot in place and simply melt, which is its usual practice in the southern areas.

When a river freezes, the thickest ice is usually at the river's edge and the thinnest where the current flows. Snow on top of a solid cover of river ice has an insulating effect, and this will slow the formation of thicker ice underneath. Consequently, if the snow is blown off a river, the cleared part will form thicker ice. River ice generally cracks when the temperature is becoming colder, due to contraction, and not, as popular belief would have it, when the weather is warming up. Ice locked to the banks of the river will crack to relieve the tension forces caused by contraction. While water entering the cracks may freeze and heal them, contraction and cracking will continue as long as the air temperature is falling.

In the late winter and early spring, the latitude of the area has a great effect on melting, as the afternoon sun is lower in the sky in the northern latitudes, and sections of the river can be shaded from the sun either by trees along the bank or by the nature of the terrain. With all these factors, it is obviously impossible to forecast when, where, or if ice jams will form on any river.

Confluences of major rivers are prone to ice jams, particularly if one of the rivers is liable to break up before the other, or if its upstream section breaks up before its own downstream section. A jam is formed when moving ice meets stationary ice, which is what happens in both of these situations. There are large flood plains near many river confluences in northern B.C. which indicate these events have happened throughout history. One such place is the juncture of the Muskwa and Fort Nelson rivers at Fort Nelson. Another was the meeting of the Nechako and Fraser rivers at Prince George, since controlled by the Kenney Dam on the Nechako.

It is the way of nature, most fortunately, that such disasters prove to be the exception rather than the rule. In two examples of major ice jams experienced by the author, freak weather incidents were the cause of the jams that affected major highway facilities. The first took place on the Fraser River at Quesnel in February 1962, and the second on the Bulkley River at Smithers in April 1966.

The Quesnel Ice Jam

The ice jam at Quesnel on the Fraser River formed on February 4, 1962. It was caused by a period of most unusual weather that affected the Fraser River for 80 miles upstream of Quesnel, which is as far as Prince George, during the preceding seven days. On January 28, 1962, the temperature at Prince George rose from below zero to a daytime maximum of 45°F, with a nighttime minimum of 40°F. This represented a record high minimum for that date.

These unusually high day and night temperatures continued for five days and nights, during which 14.9 inches of rain fell. After this there was a long spell of very cold temperatures, fluctuating from freezing (32°F) to –36°F. The crucial feature was that this mild weather and rain occurred only on this one section of the river. Downstream from Quesnel, temperatures remained cold with little precipitation, and the ice cover, initially 14 inches thick, stretched unbroken for 100 miles to the south.

As the heavy rain fell on frozen ground around Prince George, there was a low-level surge of water into the Fraser from the tributary streams in the area. The rain also weakened the ice cover on the river, and as a result, the ice broke up for 80 miles below Prince George. It all flowed downstream to meet the unbroken ice cover at Quesnel.

The ice started jamming during the night of February 3, and the next morning the floes were piled up for three miles upstream of the unbroken ice. This endangered the Fraser River Bridge at Quesnel. Measurements taken at the bridge showed the water and ice had risen overnight to a level 15 feet above normal for the time of year—and they were only 10 feet below the bottom of the bridge. Water backed up by the jam had already spread out through part of West Quesnel, flooding out an auto court, several homes and one road. The mayor declared a state of emergency.

The regional highway engineer at Prince George (the writer) was aware of the danger to the bridge, but did not realize the extent of the concerns of the people of Quesnel until their mayor, Alec Fraser, phoned him that evening. Fraser was brief but persistent in his request that the regional engineer be at the town hall at 11 a.m. the next morning for a meeting.

Wishing to scan the river from the air before the meeting, the engineer flew along the length of it between Prince George and Quesnel that morning in the only aircraft he could find, a two-seater with no cabin. His open seat behind the pilot gave him a good view of the continuous ice floes all the way down the river, as well as the ice jam, which reached its full glory in the centre of downtown Quesnel, right outside the pulp mill.

At the town hall, a huge gathering was waiting. In attendance were all the city council, most of the town's prominent citizens and every camera operator the local television station could round up. Discussion commenced forthwith, with one city council member rather hysterically demanding that the authorities immediately ask the national air force to bomb the ice jam out of existence. Rather sadly, the highways official had to reject this option, despite the intriguing possibility that it might lead to the first destruction of a Canadian pulp mill by an aerial bombardment by the Royal Canadian Air Force. The answer, he said, was to dynamite the jam with underwater charges and thus move it on. That was exactly what was being done as he spoke.

The first step was to dynamite some large ice floes, the largest of which was about 250 x 150 feet in size. A highways crew powderman set off 140 sticks of 50 percent ditching powder in seven separate charges of 20 sticks apiece at two-minute intervals. This successfully broke and weakened the large ice pad. The air temperature, meanwhile, dropped below zero.[4]

Highways employees checked the leading edge of the jam from the air and surveyed the banks from the ground. They observed that the pressure of the jam was piling the ice to heights of 15 feet, and at some points the river was over 900 feet wide (as opposed to a normal width of 500 to 600 feet at this time of year). They also noted that in places water was being squirted up between the ice. There was an open section of water near the leading edge of the jam, extending back into the jam about 200 yards. At the upstream end of this opening there was a protruding wedge of ice. This was considered a good place to start dynamiting in an attempt to help the water pressure start the ice moving.

They set off a small charge without noticeable effect and were preparing a larger charge of 60 sticks when the entire ice jam began moving. This was at 2 p.m. on February 5, by which time the jam was five miles long. The men working on it were fortunate to make their escape, scrambling ashore as the ice started moving very suddenly, quickly gaining a velocity estimated at 8 to 10 miles per hour.

This ice moved 12 miles downstream from Quesnel, breaking 14-inch-thick ice before it and coming to rest at a shallow section of the river divided by numerous islands. The river flowed around the grounded ice, the water level at Quesnel dropped 15 feet in two hours, and the river became clear of jammed ice at that point. It took one hour for the main ice pack to disappear.

The relief was short-lived, however, because by the next day the jam was seven miles long and was extending back upstream from its new location into a more restricted stretch of the river.

At 9 p.m. on February 6, the river again began to rise rapidly at Quesnel. The current was estimated to be flowing at 10 miles per hour,

These three photographs were taken from an open-cabin aircraft. Top to bottom: open water at Cottonwood Canyon a few miles south of Prince George; an open lead one mile south of town; the ice jam in Quesnel.

with the water full of slush and chunks of ice. Within 45 minutes the level rose 16 feet. A road foreman stationed at the new jam, 16 miles downstream, reported that he could hear loud crashing noises upstream. At about 11 p.m. the jam broke loose, and water and ice poured downstream. A wedge of ice, which was estimated to be 30 feet thick, preceded the flood.

At 3 a.m. this huge surge of water and ice had reached the Soda Creek Canyon, 40 miles downstream from its start point, and 52 miles from Quesnel. It therefore averaged 10 miles per hour on this movement, but as it would have lost speed steadily after its first rush, it is estimated that the 16-foot head of water behind the 30-foot ice wedge took off at a speed somewhere between 20 and 30 miles per hour.

Two reaction ferries were pulled up on the riverbank. One at Marguerite, 36 miles downstream of Quesnel, was pulled out to a spot 19 feet above normal high water. This ferry was smashed by the ice, and one pontoon was carried away. The second ferry was at Soda Creek, 47 miles downstream from Quesnel. It was lifted up away from its tie-up place and was left high and dry on a shelf of ice 20 feet thick. A third ferry was located at Big Bar, 170 miles downstream of Quesnel, and it was demolished by this ice. A steel pontoon from one of these ferries was recovered several weeks later at the mouth of the Fraser River, approximately 400 miles from Quesnel.

As a result of this experience, the highways department learned several lessons about ice jams:

1. Never trust such ice, no matter how thick or solid or immovable it may appear, unless you are quite certain that it is grounded. It can move at any second as it has tremendous pressures acting on it at all times.
2. Warn all people who are living below such an ice jam. Take every precaution to move people and property as far from the riverbank as possible. In this case the ice actually ground out the banks, at some points more than 20 feet above normal high-water level.
3. When an ice jam starts to move, the water behind it immediately starts to lose speed, the jam slows down as it goes and further stoppages or jams may form downstream. When this happens, low-lying land can be flooded instantly and drastically.

4. When dynamiting ice, look for thin ice or open water extending back from the leading edge of the ice jam, and place explosives there. Watch for signs of backed-up water, as the water pressure tends to open fissures in the ice. These are also good places to throw in explosives.

The Smithers Ice Jam

The second in our duet of ice jam disasters occurred on the Bulkley River at Smithers on Good Friday night, April 8, 1966. An initial rush of water and ice destroyed two spans of the Bulkley River Bridge, and the ice then jammed up approximately half a mile downstream of the bridge.

The jam originally was a mile in length, and it grew to two miles before highway crews blasted it out at noon on April 11. It only moved another half mile, stopping one mile below the bridge, but more blasting opened a channel through it during the evening of April 12.

At the same time as the ice jammed at Smithers, a similar jam formed at Quick, 18 miles upstream on the same river. There was another bridge here, but it was undamaged. This Quick ice jam was two miles in length

The Bulkley River Bridge at Smithers after the Good Friday ice jam of April 8, 1966. Two of the bridge's three 150-foot timber spans were swept away by the ice jam and can be seen lying on the ice. The river was filled with ice floes and is about 500 feet wide at this point.

when it first formed, and it grew to three miles in length. It remained in place until it rotted down and finally moved out on April 17.

As at Quesnel in 1962, freak weather conditions caused both these ice jams. Before the ice moved, the temperature at Smithers rose to 62°F at the airport, over 70°F in the town, from April 4 to 8. The minimum temperatures rose to 28°F. These very warm daytime temperatures, continuing as they did for five days, caused the ice to weaken and then to crack in the evening freeze-up. Heavy rain then brought a surge of local runoff into the river, which led to the final tremendous rush of water and ice, the destruction of the bridge and the ensuing ice jams.

Upstream of Smithers and Quick, many miles of the Bulkley River enjoy a southwesterly exposure and feel the maximum effect of the late-afternoon sun, which may have contributed to their early breakup. Many miles of the Telkwa River, a major tributary, are similarly affected. In addition, it is worth noting that at both Quick and Smithers, the ice jams formed upstream of sections of the river not exposed to the southwest, and therefore still covered with unbroken ice.

As the bridge at Smithers was two-thirds demolished, and as the only other access to the town was by a 50-mile detour, half of it a very poor road in the midst of the annual thaw and breakup, it was essential that the jammed-up ice at Smithers be moved out so the bridge could be replaced without delay. Fortunately there were several helicopters available at Smithers, including an eight-passenger Sikorsky, known as the "flying boxcar." Based on the experience gained at Quesnel, the provincial highway engineers decided that the best way to move this ice jam was to get the maximum amount of explosive to the right place in the least possible time. What better solution was there than to use this helicopter?[5]

Blasting crews used 40 percent dynamite in two-inch-diameter sticks, packed in black plastic sandbags, 50 pounds to a bag. These bags were tied tightly with twine. Some of the bags were fused by placing a detonator in one stick, waterproofing that stick with grease, and attaching seven feet of safety fuse that would burn at one foot per minute in water. Each bag of dynamite was lashed four ways with half-inch rope like a parcel, with a 30-foot length of rope extending from the bag. The free end of the rope was tied to the centre of a 10-foot pole. On the bags that were fused, the fuse was led out of the bag and was taped to the rope, making sure that there was lots of slack in the fuse.

To start with, two 50-pound sacks, one fused, were placed together. A good location would be 40 to 60 feet upstream of the leading edge of the ice jam, where free water could be seen through a small hole or fissure in the ice. The helicopter would hover a foot above this, and the powderman, roped to the copter, would swing out on the foot rail and push the two packages of dynamite into the water, having first lit the fuse. The current would sweep the two bags downstream under the ice, and the pole at the end of the 30-foot rope would wedge across the hole in the ice, anchoring the charges under the ice. The helicopter then left, and five or six minutes later the charge would go off.

Several hundred of these charges were set and detonated with only one misfire, which was caused when the fuse and cap were pulled out of the stick by the river's current. This was avoided afterwards by leaving more slack in the fuse.

The blasting operation was organized for mass production, with charges prepared by a crew of men on the ground, and the helicopter picking them up, shuttling them to the jam and setting them off about every 10 minutes. The charges grew in size as the work progressed, until

This worker is placing charges as the helicopter hovers.

as many as nine 50-pound packages were being placed and set off at one time, giving a total charge of 450 pounds.

The helicopter could carry a goodly number of charges, and after one set was fused it would fly away until the shot was exploded, then immediately return so the crew could fire another charge. This saved time over the original method of returning to the ground to pick up each individual charge. It was also essential that an experienced engineer ride with the helicopter and survey the jam constantly between shots, looking for pressure points in the jam and for places where backed-up water could be led in, which would add to the pressure at the leading edge of the jam.[6] This engineer would tell the powderman exactly where to place the charges.

On April 11, after four hours of the steady blasting described above, the main ice jam began to move. When it started, it all moved at once over its one-mile length, and within 45 minutes it was gone. The water flooding around the bridge fell rapidly behind it.

One incident illustrates the danger of remaining in the vicinity once the ice moves. There was a temporary trailer-mounted water pump installed near the jam by the municipality, as the regular water supply to one part of Smithers was incapacitated. When the ice started to move, two men tried to remove this pump, with neither of them realizing how much danger they were in. They backed a small truck up to the trailer

A charge goes off near the remains of the bridge in the main ice jam.

pump, and as one man was connecting the trailer, the moving ice jam stopped for a minute as large ice floes grounded in one channel. The water behind the ice instantly started to spread out and rise, and in a few seconds the truck and trailer were in quickly rising water. The truck driver put his vehicle in gear and drove away, and the man behind, caught between truck and trailer, had his leg broken.

Meanwhile, the ice still moving behind the newly grounded floes found an outlet on the far side of the river. It took off across a low-lying poplar-treed flat, bowling over large trees like ninepins. These trees made a noise like popping firecrackers as they went down. In the midst of this, a large moose appeared, running for its life. It did not make it. This author has never seen a more impressive example of the power of nature.

The ice from the main jam moved off down the river, but there was about half a mile of slush ice built up behind the jam due to the low temperatures after the first stoppage. When the initial momentum of the river slowed, this slush ice grounded below the bridge and caused a second ice jam.

It was much more difficult to dynamite this ice than it had been to blast the original jam. Removing the second ice jam was like trying to blast out a bowl of mush. Crews had to use charges totalling as much as 450 pounds, and these were ineffectual if they got too deep into the mush. The best method was to place the charges on top of the mush and sink them a few feet down so the explosion would displace as much of the slush ice as possible by splattering it all over the place. This technique, combined with a strategy of working an open lead back progressively into the mush ice, finally paid off at 5 p.m. the next day, April 12, when the crew broke an open channel up past the wrecked bridge. This channel grew progressively wider as the thick compressed ice on either side of it fell in and floated down the river.

Aerial reconnaissance indicated that the ice downstream had dispersed, and the river was clear enough at Smithers for crews to replace spans in the 290-foot gap in the bridge. This work started on April 13, with false bents being driven out from either side. (False bents are lines of piling driven to allow the truss to be assembled in place. They are removed when the truss is complete.) They were driven through an eight-foot thickness of ice at the river's edge.

The missing spans of the Bulkley River Bridge being replaced.

The experience gained at the Smithers ice jam showed that ice jams can be effectively dynamited using a large helicopter, although success in moving any jam depends on many factors, as well as luck. The major factor is the extent to which the jammed ice is subjected to pressure (i.e. the amount and head of water pressing on it). If most of the water can pass the jam, then there is less chance of moving the ice by blasting away a key section of the jam because there is no buildup of water to lift it and push it away. The amount of water in the river after the jam also determines the schedule of events. If the jam is followed by freezing temperatures and a sudden drop in water levels upstream, then more of the jammed ice will ground.

The greatest help is if the person directing the blasting has a good knowledge of the river channels in the area—or a good map. This ensures he isn't just relying on instinct when he surveys a vast carpet of jammed-up ice and has to decide where the large river channels and currents are located, and where the sandbars with grounded ice on them are. No amount of blasting will move grounded ice, but even a small charge, if placed correctly, can start a jam moving. Eventually someone will develop an electronic scanner that can spot water movement under the ice, and when such a device becomes available, blasting ice jams will depend less on luck than it must at present. Cool nerves, resourceful thinking and determination will still be necessary, however, particularly in your powderman and helicopter pilot.

In relation to the last comment, an event not recorded in the official account bears telling. On one occasion the helicopter landed on a spur of ice frozen to the bottom. The crew was going to place three bundles of explosives under the floating ice nearby, which would take some time, so the pilot shut down the rotor. After they were done, the two engineers, one of whom was the regional highway engineer,[7] returned to the helicopter. They were followed by the powderman after he had lit the fuses to the three large charges.[8] The pilot started the engine and engaged the main rotor. It immediately emitted a large cloud of jet-black smoke, and the pilot announced he would have to shut down the engine—even though the fuses were burning!

The powderman was equal to the challenge. He immediately announced to all in the cabin that there was lots of time and he was going to return to the charges to extinguish the fuses. Steadily, carefully and without undue haste, he did just that. There was still about half of the seven-foot fuse remaining on the last charge he defused. It was slow-burning fuse! He was the kind of powderman anyone would be pleased to work with again. The pilot realized he had forgotten to release the brake on his rotor when he started up. After he had loosened the brake and made some adjustments, he started the engine and rotor before the fuses were relit (after they were replaced with standard length fuse). The blasting was completed successfully.[9]

Snow and Ice on the Roadway

It doesn't seem right to leave the subject of weather and roads in British Columbia without saying something about removing snow and ice from the roadway, that sometimes mundane, sometimes monotonous, but occasionally quite exciting chore for the men and women who look after our roads.

Before it was privatized in 1987, the B.C. Department of Highways boasted staff that made it one of the leading North American agencies in the development of specialized snow removal and sanding equipment for trucks and graders. This is especially surprising when you consider that the history of snowplowing (elitists will say "ploughing") in the province didn't begin until the 1920s, and there wasn't a fully effective service province-wide until the 1950s.

From 1920 to the mid-1940s there were no high mountain passes or very difficult sections, such as the Fraser Canyon, kept open in the winter. This was because the Fraser Canyon road was closed for the winter during these years, and there were no roads within most of the high passes known to us now. Allison Pass was bereft of a road, and so were Rogers, Kootenay and Pine passes. The road over Monashee Pass, between Vernon and Nakusp, was closed down when the snow piled up.

The early road-maintenance staff in the Kootenay districts, particularly the West Kootenay area looked after from Nelson, tried to keep open the most vital of its difficult, narrow and winding roads for at least some of the time after the end of October. Between 1925 and 1935, only three of the 10 winters had less than heavy snow and ice conditions, and the poor economic conditions of that period did little to help that.

The willing and much-loved mechanical beast of burden in these years was the Cat 60 tractor, the first of which appeared in Nelson in 1929. It surpassed any of the tractors, or trucks, available then (trucks had just solid rubber tires a few years earlier), and few had what the Cat 60 in Nelson had then—a heated cab and "non-freeze mixtures" in its radiator and engine cooling system. It was ahead of its time and was remembered by its users with affection long after larger, and supposedly better, machines came on the market. It saved the day.

The district engineer in Nelson in 1929 was William Ramsay, and Bill was one of the best of the breed. His practice was to send out the Cat 60 with at least two operators on snowplowing trips, which often lasted six weeks before they returned to base. They would take a light truck with housing on its deck called "the caboose." It contained two cots and a wood stove. The operators lived on the road, were supplied on the road and plowed as they went. They slept and ate in the caboose, although members of the public would often offer them a meal and at times a bed as well.

If you were unlucky enough to have a heavy snowstorm right after they passed, you sometimes had to wait a month or so for relief, although they would back up for vital sections. Bill Ramsay visited them often, at least once a week, and he always brought snacks and hot drinks. The operators were always happy to hear his broad Scots accent, which he kept until the day he died.

Some comments in the district reports for that era are illuminating. In the report for 1930 for Revelstoke district, which also came under Ramsay, was the observation: "One hundred and fifty miles were snow ploughed, but it was found, owing to the exceptional conditions, impossible to keep portions open throughout the winter." For other areas it was the same story, and often all they kept open were the roads to the railway. The year 1932 saw another heavy snowfall, and it was reported that the southern trans-provincial highway in the Elk Valley approaching Fernie was closed from January to April by a huge snowslide.

Bill Ramsay joined the Department of Public Works when the position of district engineer was introduced in the early 1920s. He remained in Nelson when the Conservatives took power provincially in 1928, but not when the Liberals returned to office in 1933. Effective April 1, 1934, most engineering districts were reorganized, and many

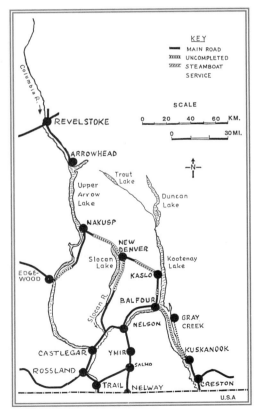

Bill Ramsay's District: This map, taken from a larger one in the Minister of Public Works' 1925 annual report, shows the Nelson engineering district.

Up until 1934 it included Nelson, Creston, Rossland-Trail, Kaslo-Slocan and Revelstoke electoral districts. By the end of 1930, all the uncompleted road sections shown on the map were finished, including some sections of very difficult work on lakeside cliffs. The circuit north and south of Nelson through Balfour, New Denver, Castlegar, Trail and Salmo, with its offshoots, amounted to about 300 miles of road. Plowing all that in the 1930s in a heavy-snow winter with a small tractor could take six weeks.

Bill maintained 30 miles west from Revelstoke, 20 miles west from Edgewood, 10 miles west from Rossland and 16 miles east from Creston.

district engineers relocated. Ramsay was moved to Williams Lake, and Evan Jones, the district engineer at Cranbrook, took over the Nelson/Creston district (he became deputy minister after the war). In 1938 Bill Ramsay was relocated again, this time to Kamloops, where he stayed until he retired in 1948. When the Highway Board was formed by public works minister Herbert Anscomb in 1941, Ramsay became a member, the only district engineer so honoured, and he remained on the board until 1946.

The late 1940s and the 1950s saw the emergence of what we now know as a fully effective winter maintenance service. A lineup of new snowplows and sanding trucks, all mechanically equipped for snow and ice removal by the Department of Public Works and photographed outside the Allison Pass depot at the opening of the Hope-Princeton Highway on November 2, 1949, showed their good intentions for that highway. It was rather sad that, on that same day, in the late hours of the night, an unexpected arrival of black ice caused the first fatality on the new highway.

The department had to wait until 1952 for its second winter challenge, the John Hart Peace River Highway (to use its full name) that crossed the Rocky Mountains by way of Pine Pass. DPW established a depot 18 miles south of the summit at Honeymoon Creek. At that elevation, it was often necessary to dig out the windows after extreme winter snowfalls, as the piled-up snow would gradually cover them as the winter progressed. The department also installed in-floor heating in

Snowplows and sanding trucks are seen outside the Allison Pass depot. On November 2, 1949, the day the Hope-Princeton Highway opened, black ice caused the highway's first fatality.

the workshops, which made life much easier. It was a happy camp, the only problem being the food-seeking black bears around the kitchen.

The next real test was the opening of the Salmo-Creston highway through Kootenay Pass in 1966 (elevation 5,820 feet). This was where the department really started dealing with avalanches as well as snow and ice. Later on, of course, Coquihalla Pass was added.

In the earlier decades there was a special comradeship among users of the roads in winter, especially in the more remote areas and through the mountains, a reassuring feature sadly lacking today. The author experienced this in the course of his duties as district engineer in 1950. In those years, for easier winter travel most drivers preferred to cross the Canada/U.S. border at Cascade, cross the Columbia River on the ferry at Northport, Washington, and then re-enter British Columbia at Waneta. In this way they avoided the very difficult section of the old road between Cascade and Rossland, with its two summits. (That driver's nightmare is now replaced by the modern highway from Christina Lake and Bonanza summit straight through to Castlegar.)

On this particular winter evening, the author left the Boundary district en route to Nelson by car too late to cross the U.S. border before it closed at 8 p.m. As he drove up to the first summit between Cascade and Rossland, it started snowing heavily, and soon there were many inches of snow on the road. He carefully parked by the roadside and started to put on chains, regretting that he had misplaced his gloves because his hands kept freezing—so much so that he had to repeatedly retreat to the car to thaw them out. He was in the midst of doing this when the Greyhound bus arrived, and the bus driver stopped, as most drivers did then in winter when they saw someone in distress. Leaving his cab, with gloves on, the bus driver told our unequipped motorist to go into the bus and warm up. Then the bus driver himself put the chains on, wished his fellow driver good luck and left. This author was warmed by more than the heater's blast. On arrival at Rossland he took steps to close the road until the snowplows could get there at break of day. (It is interesting to note that in the early days of motor transport, the Greyhound Bus Company ran its own snowplows in parts of Canada, including southern B.C.)

Another incident, which occurred in central B.C. on the main road there, the Northern Trans-Provincial Highway, shows how drivers helped each other. One sunny Sunday morning in mid-winter in the late 1950s, the author was driving between Burns Lake and Houston when he came upon a familiar scene in those days: a hilly section of road with ice on the surface and sunshine slicking it up. There were five cars at the bottom of the hill, and the drivers were conferring on what to do as they had repeatedly tried to drive up the hill and all of them had slid back down. The slickest section on the hill was only about 100 yards long, so the author, who had a hand shovel with him, moved some snow and scraped the frozen earth beneath it to gather enough material to lay on the ice. Then the drivers, together, pushed each car up the hill, and all went on their way with cheery farewells.

Instead of community effort, we now have more efficient procedures and equipment for snowplowing and sanding. The best units are usually road graders fitted with front-mounted vee plows or with snow-blowing equipment, and heavy gravel trucks fitted with sand bodies, spreaders and front-mounted blade plows or underbody plows. The sanding trucks also have instruments that measure the road surface temperature and mix chemicals into the sand as needed.

The underbody plow, a plow blade and mechanism fitted under the middle of the truck, was a specialty of the B.C. highways department. It designed and made its own units, which were generally much better than those commercially available. The homemade machines were more rugged and more suitable for the special requirements of B.C.'s mountain areas. The department also modifed front-mounted plows to throw the snow far into the right-of-way and over roadside snowbanks while plowing at high speed. This required superior trucks with increased power, which the department obtained as special orders from truck manufacturers

The best way to plow a heavy snowfall on a two-lane mountain road is with a road grader equipped with snow blades and a snow blower.

in B.C. The logging industry's need for very powerful trucks helped out in this. The department's production shops were at Cloverdale on the Mainland, and at Langford on Vancouver Island.

It is common practice to spread sand and grit on roadways for better traction on snow and ice, and salt or calcium chloride are universally added to melt ice, although there is continuing debate about the extent of vehicle damage caused by these chemicals. Urea would also melt

The workhorse of snowplowing and sanding in B.C. is a two-axle truck with a sand-spraying hopper, front-mounted snow blade and an underbody blade mounted between the axles.

ice, but it is so expensive that it never caught on. Another method of removing ice or packed snow is simply to scrape it off, which is where underbody plows or graders excel. The blades have serrated edges for better cutting into the ice, and the underbody position enables hydraulic arms to apply downward pressure using the vehicle weight. For work closer to the pavement surface, the blade is changed to one with a straight edge or a rubber bottom edge.

The state-of-the-art snowplow and sanding truck with the four gas cylinders behind the cab, shown on page 103, was a special project of the Mechanical Branch of the Ministry of Transportation and Highways in the early 1980s and was on display at Expo 86. Produced by the branch in cooperation with the Cummins Engine Company of Columbus, Indiana, and Mogas Fuel Systems of Vancouver, B.C., it was powered by a six-cylinder turbocharged engine running on a mixture of 80 percent compressed natural gas and 20 percent diesel oil.

The branch and its partners gained valuable information on cylinder head temperatures and pressures in such an engine, using a transducer introduced between the cylinder head and the cylinder body. They also studied the effect of turbocharging on engine operation using the alternative fuel mixture and established optimum diesel-compressed natural gas ratios, fuel usage, power output, etc., during dynamometer tests.

As well as the gas tanks shown, the vehicle has four smaller steel gas tanks side-mounted, all maintained at 3000 psi, as well as a 50-gallon diesel tank, and the engine can be switched to run on diesel only. The truck, which is a combined snowplow and sander with front-mounted and underbody plows, has a range of 100 miles on the diesel/gas mixture and is equipped with a microcomputer, electric over hydraulic valves, and onboard load cells.[10]

In mechanical engineering, as in all science, nothing ventured is nothing gained, and as alternative fuels for vehicles become more viable, it is hard to find a better testing environment for a truck engine under all conditions than sanding and snowplowing. In addition, in 1985 the ministry converted the Albion–Fort Langley ferry, the MV *Klatawa*, to run on compressed natural gas and diesel, the first known ferry to be so powered. So in addition to studying the mixture under the stress and strain of a snowplow engine, they could now examine its performance in the steady long use of a ferry engine. Unfortunately, when the Mechanical Branch subsequently disappeared during the Vander Zalm government's privatization of the highway department in the mid-1980s, such innovative government research as the cng/diesel projects on land and water became a thing of the past.

In the last count on record before privatization, one made in the year 1980, the British Columbia Ministry of Transportation and Highways operated the following complement of snow- and ice-removal equipment: 900 blade plows mounted on trucks; 150 graders with snow wings; 31 rotary snowplows; 850 tailgate or pull sanders; 130 truck-body-mounted sanders. With this equipment they maintained 25,476 miles of primary and secondary roads within the province. In the course of privatization, much of this excellent equipment went on sale at fire sale prices, and the well-equipped garages and workshops throughout the province that had maintained it were leased out or put on the block. Such are the wonders of privatization. The roads, however, are still being sanded and the snow is still being plowed.

The State-of-the-Art Plow and Sand Truck, 1986

Built for the new Coquihalla Highway, this uniquely equipped vehicle was designed to meet the challenge of heavy snowfalls and severe icing conditions found in the Coquihalla Pass. In this snowplow and sanding truck, the operator can, with the flick of a switch on the top-of-the-windscreen control panel, lift, lower or roll over the front plow and set it to "float," lift or lower the underbody plow; hoist or lower the sand body; start the conveyor to the rear sand spinner or the second conveyor to the left side spinner; adjust the speed of either spinner; or switch one or the other to automatic at either low, medium or high.

The onboard microcomputer then takes over and adjusts the rate of sand or salt dispersal to suit the truck speed, weighs the sand or salt load constantly by the load cells, compares lessening load volume to estimated spread, records load depletion and warns the driver when less than 10 percent of the load remains. It notes excess fuel consumption and measures mileage as it records sand or salt use.

The system is self-calibrating, and the conveyor speeds are infinitely variable through the electric over hydraulic drive, which is constantly adjusted by the computer that drives the hydraulic valves and monitors the load cells, recording and showing results and functions underway on the LCD display. The operator can, again by flicking a switch, give a special blast of sand at an intersection. He monitors outside temperatures (shown on his control panel) and adjusts the amount of salt spread to suit. He changes special driving and safety-light patterns on the truck by means of an illuminated switch light control panel—with special light patterns for front plowing, underbody plowing, sanding or backing up. The mechanical material delivery system, conveyors, spinners, hoppers, etc., and the underbody plow were designed and built by the Langford Depot of the B.C. Ministry of Transportation and Highways. The Equipment Branch of the ministry's Victoria headquarters conceived and planned the entire system including the computer-activated feature.[11]

This was a quite remarkable refinement to a vital piece of highway snow and ice removal equipment, completed very shortly before the branch was dismantled by the privatization program introduced by Premier Bill Vander Zalm.

CHAPTER 5

THE OTHER B.C. FERRIES

*These ferries are part of the highways ministry and were part
of British Columbia's history from the very beginning.*

*I*t was only in the last two decades of the 19th century that
settlement in British Columbia started to spread out from the coastal
centres and inland mining camps. Served initially by a most inadequate
road system with few bridges over streams of any size, there were at one
time a total of 140 crossings of rivers, lakes or ocean inlets served by
ferries. These early ferries were a wonderful example of privatization, as
almost all of these services were privately operated. However, the use of
government-operated ferries steadily increased, and finally they greatly
outnumbered the private operations. The latter either charged too much
or did not have the funds to upgrade in size when necessary.

It was not until the first two decades of the 20th century had passed
that the road authority followed the example of the railways with their
trestles and trusses and put to good use the remarkable qualities of
native Douglas fir timbers in the making of good bridges. (This change
was also brought about by the advent of district road engineers in 1919.)
The oversupply of ferries was also reduced by the building of new roads
and by the relocation of existing roads.

One of the earliest ferries on record was at Spuzzum, on the Fraser
River, where a flat-bottomed punt operated from 1858 to 1863 until it
was displaced by the Alexandra Bridge. Another ferry route crossed

the same river at New Westminster, going back and forth from 1884 to 1904. The first ferry, the *K. de K.*, was replaced by the *Surrey* in 1891. This service was operated by the City of New Westminster.

By 1925 the number of ferry crossings was down to 54. There were four private vessels, and of the 50 government-operated ferries, 30 were pontoon reaction ferries propelled by the force of the current (described later), 8 were gas-propelled boats, 1 was steam propelled, 6 were cable-driven scows and 5 were rowboats or canoes. By 1973 there were 36 ferry routes employing 34 government-operated ferries and 6 subsidized vessels, and the number of reaction ferries was down to 9, mostly due to bridge or road construction. (Certain routes had more than one ferry operating on them.) There were no rowboats or canoes. During the fiscal year ending March 31, 1973, the fleet carried over two million vehicles and over six million passengers, including vehicle drivers. By 1985, just before the ferry service lost all its coastal routes to the BC Ferry Corporation, the number of routes was the same, but the number of reaction ferries was down to six. That year the fleet carried 3.9 million vehicles and 8.9 million passengers. In a way, these statistics are a fairly good measure of the growth of B.C.

In the first 50 years of the life of the province, numerous sternwheel-driven steamers were active in its waters. These were all owned by private individuals or companies, particularly the Canadian Pacific Railway, and they plied the rivers, lakes and estuaries of British Columbia most diligently. Many times they provided a ferry service, particularly on the coast, but they and their adventures have been well described elsewhere, as has the story of the BC Ferries system started in 1960. The tales told here are about "the other B.C. ferries."

Basket Ferries

For a description of the most basic ferry of all, that run by human power, we are indebted to Dennis Swan of Victoria. He is the son of Hamilton Lindsay Swan, who was the engineer in charge of replacing the Alexandra Bridge across the Fraser River at Spuzzum between 1924 and 1926. To get across the river while the bridge was under construction, they used a ferry. In contrast to the original ferry at that site before the first bridge was built, this one was an aerial basket ferry, fully operative when Dennis and his mother and father arrived there early in 1924.[1]

First, a little historical background. When the CPR opened its transcontinental line in 1886, it sketchily replaced the historic wagon road running beside the line through the Fraser Canyon with a one-lane road with flimsy wood trestles at the water's edge. This road got very little use, and when the 1894 flood took out most of the trestles and the Alexandra Bridge, it was a great relief to the CPR. The little-used road was simply a nuisance to the railwaymen, particularly when they were plowing snow, although its loss was something of a blow to those wishing to travel by any means other than rail.

One of the bridge's cable anchorages was damaged in the flood, and as a result the deck was twisted so badly that no vehicles could use it. It was only good for foot traffic or horse riders from then on, as was the road, which became a trail. Some time between 1910 and 1924, when we have Swan's account of it, the government obviously installed a basket ferry, which provided pedestrian access between Spuzzum, with its general store and a few houses, and Boston Bar, the larger settlement located about 10 miles upstream. The ultimate conveyance was the North Bend aerial ferry, installed much later and shown and described in the photograph and text on page 107.

In 1924 the ferry basket was made of wood and was about six feet by six feet in dimension, with sideboards and with a framework at either end about six feet high. Each frame had a pulley at the top. Both pulleys rested on a carrier cable that stretched between two towers, one either side of the river. There was a second cable, or rope, running through the basket framework and anchored to each side of the river. The basket could carry up to four persons, and one or more of the passengers had to pull the ferry across, hand over hand, using that rope.

The first half of the trip was easy; the basket ran down the catenary of the carrying cable propelled by the force of gravity. It was pulling it up the second half that was hard work. When the basket reached the landing platform on the far side, the passengers would hook the basket to the platform and debark. Then, as instructed by a sign, they would unhook the empty basket and let it run down to the bottom of the sag of the cable, where it remained till the next passengers arrived.

The North Bend Aerial Ferry

The North Bend aerial ferry across the Fraser Canyon served traffic moving from Boston Bar to North Bend, a small settlement on the west side of the river. It was unique in Canada, and possibly anywhere, because it could carry one car or light truck. Without a vehicle it took up to 40 passengers. It went into service in March 1940 and operated until January 1986, when it was replaced by a bridge. It was a toll ferry for the first seven years of its life, and it operated for 45 years without a serious mishap.

When the ferry started service, the Fraser Canyon Road was closed every year from November 1 to March 31, preventing the arrival of any vehicles from outside the area, except for those carried in by one of the two railways. Until winter road access was restored later in the 1940s, the ferry was said to carry mainly foot passengers in the winter months, people seeking groceries across the river or visiting to play bridge. Nonetheless, in the first year it carried 3,482 cars, 472 light trucks and 24,942 passengers. The length of the crossing was 429 yards, and the ferry took three minutes to cross.

In the 1970s the ferry was completely renovated, with new cables and new overhead travelling gear. The refit was supervised by an engineer experienced in ski lifts.

There was a third cable that was attached to the basket and ran through two sheaves, one on either side of the river. This made it possible for someone to pull the empty basket to either side of the river when it was needed. This arrangement was necessary because there was no ferryman. Dennis Swan remembers one time when there was a heavy fog on the river. His father started pulling in the ferry from its resting place midriver, but he found it very hard pulling, and when he relaxed his grip for a second, the rope took off away from him. It was not until he had done this several times that he realized someone across the river was duplicating his efforts, unseen in the fog.

This was one of several basket ferries over the Fraser, including one that operated at Soda Creek from 1902 onwards, a great boon to the users of the Cariboo Road. Another of the early Fraser River basket ferries was put in place due to the delay in finishing the railway bridge at Cisco during the CPR main line construction. The basket ran down a steeply angled cable and was pulled back up by a man with a horse (on land). The downbound basket landed in a large pile of hay, which brought it to a soft landing (and also, no doubt, fed the horse). A user in 1884 was Jessie Ann Smith, who became well known as Widow Smith of Spence's Bridge. She used it along with Mr. and Mrs. Andrew Onderdonk, who lived near her for a while in that village.[2]

There was a basket ferry operated by a ferryman at Gravelle over the Quesnel River. In this case, the power cable came into the basket and wrapped around a drum that was turned by a large hand-operated wheel. This wheel was placed between two facing seats in the basket. The ferryman sat in the one facing ahead, and a willing passenger, usually an adult male, sat in the other facing him. Both turned the wheel together. This operation had a rather checkered career. It seemed that the most regular patron was a large gentleman who often travelled back and forth to the beer parlour in Quesnel. He was fine outbound, when he helped to operate the ferry, but on the return journey late at night (when he was required to compensate the ferryman modestly) he was not as good. Not only could he not physically perform, but once they got midriver and the basket swung sideways, as it always did, he had a habit of throwing up. In these circumstances the ferryman's dedication to public service faced its toughest test.

Reaction Ferries

The reaction ferry was the workhorse for crossing rivers in the early days, and British Columbians had many rivers to cross. The inventor of this ingenious way of moving across a river is not known, at least not to this author, but a hearty vote of thanks is due him (or her) in this corner of the world.

The first reaction ferries were simply scows. Then two pontoons were used, about 40 feet in length, spaced 20 to 24 feet apart and held in place by a wooden deck. The side-fenced deck stretched fully across the pontoons and extended a further two to three feet on either side. It accommodated one or two lanes of traffic, as well as a small cabin used by the ferryman. The pontoons were originally wooden, but later versions were made of steel.

Two towers placed on either side of the river were of sufficient height to support a cable crossing between them. At its lowest point, the cable cleared the river surface at high water by at least eight feet. On this cable there was a wheeled trolley to which was attached a second cable that ran from the bow of each pontoon, through pulleys and over a drum in the cabin.

When the ferry was ready to start, lying at its landing facing upstream, the operator would cast off and place the vessel at an angle to the river current by using a paddle board or by adjusting the cable. The current hitting the inshore-inclined side of both pontoons pushed the ferry both downstream and across the river. The overhead cable resisted the downstream thrust, and the sideways thrust propelled both the ferry and the trolley across the river to the landing on the other side. To take

Left: The *Usk* reaction ferry in action with its rescue boat. This photo was taken in June 1980.
Right: The *Marguerite* reaction ferry approaches its landing. It crosses the Fraser River beside the Cariboo Highway and is located near the site of the old Hudson's Bay Company's Fort Alexandria.

the ferry back across the river, the process was carried out in reverse. The benefit of pontoons was that they gave two sides for the water to react against instead of the one provided by a scow.

This mode of transportation is silent, pollution free and requires no fuel. It does, however, require a steady and fairly powerful river current. Back eddies at the landings are the enemy. It was a very simple and workable system, and one that was ideal for remote locations within the British Columbia Interior. That reaction ferries were used for so many years is proof of this. At one time there were 22 reaction ferries crossing the Fraser River, and as late as 1991 there were still six of them in use in the province—three on the Fraser River, two on the North Thompson River and one on the Skeena River.

There are many tales about reaction ferries, of which a few stand out in the writer's mind. The first is of the Isle Pierre ferry on the Nechako River a few miles from Prince George. The Department of Public Works provided a house alongside the crossing for the ferryman and his family at a modest rent. As always, it was on the town side of the river.

This ferryman had an unfortunate habit of sleeping in, to the intense frustration of the early-morning ferry users living on the other side of the river who needed the ferry to get to work. When he slept in several days in a row, one user lost patience completely and brought a rifle with him one morning. Finding the ferry on the far side unattended once again, he fired a shot across the river into the peak of the ferry house, which effectively did the job. When he repeated the process a few days later, the ferryman suddenly appeared, also with a rifle, and fired back! Nearby neighbours called the police and the RCMP settled the matter.

A reaction ferry that crossed the Columbia River at Trail from 1895 to 1912 had the dubious distinction of being the most fatal to its ferrymen. It was run by the smelter and the government, and it killed one ferryman by a blow from the winch handle and another by drowning. Another time it broke away, and when a passerby shouted, "Get a boat!" the ferryman replied, "A boat be damned. Get a bridge!" They did.

The next of these tales relates to the reaction ferry at Cedarvale, a small settlement alongside the Skeena River in northern British Columbia some miles upstream of Terrace. Part of this tiny community is on the other bank of the river from the road, and the ferry served the residents for many long years and, before them, the pioneer religious community of Minskinish. The ferry ceased service in 1975 when it ran aground after breaking away when the tower collapsed in high water. The passengers were rescued by a helicopter. Quite soon after there was a bridge at Kitwanga, only a few miles away, and the residents used that.

The Skeena is probably the strongest-flowing river over a long distance in British Columbia, and Cedarvale is on its section of greatest activity, immediately upstream of the Kitselas Canyon. The sternwheeler *Mount Royal* was blown broadside to the current in that canyon in 1907 during one of its trips. It capsized and was never seen again.

This canyon is the worst hazard on the river, and one Cedarvale ferryman can attest to that. One day he was relaxing in the ferry cabin when he spied what he thought was a raft of logs floating along in the current with a man standing on top of it. The man was waving wildly for help as he knew he would never survive in the nearby canyon, which he was approaching at a high rate of speed.

The ferryman immediately jumped into the small boat with an outboard motor that was tied up at the landing, put there for just such use, cast off, reached the raft and rescued the man. When he asked about the logs, it turned out this was not a raft of logs at all. It was the load of a logging truck that was suspended under the logs, attached to them by the load tie-downs and travelling along with them under the water like a submarine. The truck had left the road some miles upstream, and the driver had left the cab when it sank into the river. He had climbed up on top of his load to stay out of the water, and he was thankful that he was carrying cedar logs and not others of greater weight. All of it went into the canyon, the logs reappearing downstream. The truck was never seen again.

The final reaction-ferry story involves the Lytton reaction ferry, which operated in such a strong current on the Fraser River that it required two ferrymen. On May 3, 1979, it broke its main cable and took off downstream with ferrymen and passengers aboard. Fortunately the outboard motor of the towed rescue boat started at once, and all the people on the ferry reached shore safely. A forestry department tug that was nearby escorted the drifting ferry downstream to Boston Bar, where it was beached, disassembled, trucked back to Lytton, reassembled and put back into service after both steel pontoons had been lengthened. It also acquired a new lifeboat, a Zodiac Mark III with an electric start.[3]

Cable Ferries

The power-cable ferry was used for relatively short crossings of slow-moving rivers or lake narrows. This type of ferry is a barge that pulls itself across the water on an underwater shore-to-shore cable, powered by an onboard engine and winch. It carries many more vehicles than a reaction ferry does.

Cable ferries have movable hinged aprons at each end, and when docking they pull themselves in, head-on, to a sloping ramp. The apron is then lowered and the vehicles drive up the ramp. These ramps were first made of wood or gravel, but finally all of them were made of concrete.

In 1938 there were six cable ferries operating in the province: one at Castlegar; two over the Columbia River (at 12 miles and 24 miles from Revelstoke); one at Harrop and one at Nelson, both of which crossed the West Arm of Kootenay Lake; and one at Needles over the narrows between the two Arrow Lakes. A number of years ago the Nelson ferry was replaced by a bridge. The one at Needles became a self-propelled ferry for a while, but became a cable ferry once again in 1990, and the government acquired another of this type of ferry for a crossing of the Kootenay River at Glade. Over the years there has also been a cable ferry, guided by an overhead cable and propelled by paddles, that crossed the Kootenay River at West Creston. A short-lived hovercraft cable ferry at Fort Nelson suffered fire damage early in its life and was not replaced.

The cable ferry installed at Needles is the largest, with a 40-car capacity, and its 5,000-foot-long cable is the longest in North America. Not bad for a ferry that started off as a launch and a raft in 1924. The Castlegar ferry has been the leader so far in total annual traffic carried.

There are many stories told of these ferries, and a most amusing incident took place on the first day of 1950 at Nelson. It happened very early in the day—in the small hours of the morning in fact. After the ferry had come to rest on the ramp late the night before, on Hogmanay, it seemed that a New Year's Eve celebration of sorts took place—after all, it was the start of the second half of the century. Just before the last of the celebrants left, early in the morning, one of them, who had celebrated extensively, thought it would be amusing to climb down inside the scow, open the scuttle plug in the bottom of the ferry and let the water in. This he did, and then he went on his way.

The water came in very slowly, and it was not until long after everyone had gone that the ferry settled down completely onto the ramp. The water at these ramps is shallow, only a few feet deep, so even when the ferry was right down on the bottom, most of the deck and all of the superstructure were still above water. It was just a little waterlogged at the stern, although the inside of the scow was nearly full.

When the head ferryman arrived later in the morning to start the service, he panicked, apparently not understanding clearly what had happened. Not knowing what else to do, he called the police and the fire brigade.

The fire chief immediately started up all his pumps and diligently commenced pumping out the water. By this time quite a crowd had gathered, and after about half an hour of pumping, a man, apparently more perceptive than most, sidled up to the fire chief and asked him how long he thought it would take to pump out Kootenay Lake! The plug was replaced, the pumping restarted and the ferry was soon back in service, after it had a chance to dry out.

This was not the first sinking of the Nelson ferry, an earlier version of which made its inaugural trip in September 1913. In December 1946, in a fierce storm with driving snow, the ferry, which in that period was a wooden scow, took on excess water in the bilges because it was driven at high speed. It reached the ramp before foundering, and, according to the Vancouver *Province* of November 20, 1946, "the offshore end of the ferry was all that was submerged." These ramps were truly havens for all these partial sinkings. The wooden scow was replaced by a steel one in October 1948.

The next story involves a cable ferry that was not in B.C. but very close to it—only a few hundred feet south of the border in Porthill, Idaho, where there is a crossing of the Kootenai River (the American name) just a few miles from Creston, B.C. Almost as Canadian as American, the residents of Porthill find themselves much closer to Creston than they are to their county centre, Bonners Ferry. A certain amount of intermarriage, a lot of intercommunication and, more than anything, the fact that many Crestonites much preferred the business hours of the Porthill tavern to those of B.C. beer parlours brought these international neighbours together, or at least did so some years ago when the events described here occurred.

The J.H. Huscroft Co., a logging company in Creston, held cutting licences for timber in the Selkirk Mountains near the international boundary, just west of the Kootenay River. This timber could only be reached via roads in the United States, and the company had to use the Porthill ferry to haul logs to their sawmill in Creston. One afternoon a rather ancient logging truck, loaded down with these cooperatively handled logs and driven by a young Canadian driver, pulled onto the ferry at its western landing, across the river from Porthill.

The truck was the first vehicle on, and the driver left the engine running after he stopped on the deck of the ferry. He had been having trouble with his starter, and he carefully placed the truck in neutral before he climbed out of the cab to stretch his legs. Two cars followed, and in a few minutes the ferry got underway with a jerk, as cable ferries often do. The truck's gear lever slipped into low gear, and the vehicle slowly started moving. There was nothing between it and the river but an open deck, a light chain barrier and the apron of the ferry.

Unfortunately, as soon as the truck had gone a few feet, the proximity of the winch house's wall to the side of the truck made it impossible for the driver to get to the door on the driver's side. As the door on the other side was locked, and the keys were in the ignition in the truck, all that the driver could do was look on helplessly.

When the truck reached the apron, which was only slightly raised, its weight forced down the front of the vessel, until, in stately fashion, the truck rolled and slid into the water. The ferry bobbed up again after the weight left. The truck ended up only a few feet under water, floating directly in front of the ferry and with most of the cab above water, held there by the flotation of the logs. Everything was being slowly moved ahead by the ferry.

The ferry operator stopped his vessel and strolled over to look at the situation. He picked up the two chains that had been brushed aside by the truck and were still attached on either side of the apron. He leaned forward, looped each of them around the log tie-downs and snubbed them up to keep the truck in place. Then he went back to his controls and restarted the ferry. With the truck preceding it, the vessel slowly resumed its trip across the river. There was a good depth of water to float the truck in as the river was in flood.

When they reached the other side and the truck's front wheels touched the river bottom, the ferryman stopped the ferry and unhooked the truck. Then he used his skiff to go ashore, started up an ancient bulldozer kept there to grade the gravel ramps, chained the tractor to the truck, towed the vehicle up the ramp and parked it right across the street from the tavern. He then docked the ferry and unloaded the cars from it, which of course contained the truck driver's fascinated fellow travellers.

All of this had come to the attention of the patrons of the tavern, being clearly visible through the windows. They spilled out onto the street to offer both advice and derision to the young driver, adding hugely to his embarrassment. Red in the face, he struggled to start the engine after he had mopped it all over and watched water pour from it for some time. He cranked it and cranked it, with a starter which miraculously worked, until, to the surprise of all, the engine burst into life, and off he went, leaving one more story to be told over the beer from then on.

Self-Propelled Ferries

This leaves us with the aristocrats of the Interior and Coast ferries, the self-propelled or "certified" vessels (the certification coming from Canada's Department of Transport). We turn to the Interior ferries first, which ran on the major lakes—in order of size, Arrow (Upper and Lower), Kootenay, Okanagan, Shuswap and Francois—and this brings us to the pioneers of navigation in British Columbia, the sternwheelers. These great vessels moved people on all the above-mentioned lakes except Francois, although most did not move vehicles. The exceptions were the SS *Nasookin* on Kootenay Lake and the *Sicamous* for a few years on Okanagan Lake.

Before looking at sternwheelers as ferries, let us glance at the very early days on B.C.'s lake waters as described by that renowned relater of early travel, Newton H. Chittenden, in his *Travels in British Columbia*, published in 1882. Chittenden was travelling from Vernon (which at that time was known as Priest's Valley) to Kamloops via Sicamous in 1882. There was a gap in the road system from Sicamous along Shuswap Lake to Salmon Arm, and the traveller was thoughtfully provided service by one of the sternwheelers on Shuswap Lake, the SS *Spallumcheen*, which, along with its sister ship the *Peerless*, helped greatly in the construction of the CPR transcontinental line. (The *Spallumcheen* was a jack of all trades, and for the period before the road was completed it might be said to have been the first general-purpose sternwheeler to become an integral part of the highway system.)

Chittenden joined the boat at Fortune's Landing, now known as Enderby, continuing on via the Shuswap River to Shuswap Lake at Sicamous, where he spent the night. He describes moving out on the lake, bound for Salmon Arm, in the early morning, a deer swimming ahead, and the boat cleaving its way through dozens of salmon and trout fully visible in the pure clear water. There were also numbers uncounted of geese, ducks and swans. Oh, how bountiful nature was in the early days!

After the Canadian Pacific Railway completed its Crows Nest Railway from Fort Macleod to Kootenay Landing at the southern extremity of Kootenay Lake in 1898, it started a train ferry service from the south end of the lake to a landing called Procter on the West Arm. In 1913 it launched the sternwheeler SS *Nasookin* to serve the route. That vessel became one of the heroes of early public transportation in B.C.

In 1930 the CPR replaced the over-water link with a rail line along the west side of the main lake. At that time the province leased *Nasookin* until 1933, when it bought the steamer outright for use as a ferry. It also carried vehicles, with a capacity of one bus or large truck and

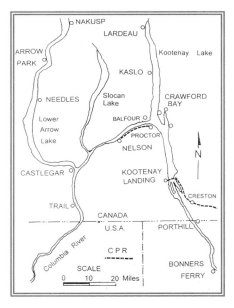

The Arrow, Slocan and Kootenay lakes area prior to 1930

30 cars. As described in chapter 2, the provincial government had built a road up the east side of the lake and needed a means to move people and vehicles across Kootenay Lake from the end of that road to a road on the West Arm of the lake leading to Nelson. The *Nasookin* was moved over to fill this need, and it ran from Gray Creek, the northern end of the lake road, to Fraser's Landing on the West Arm road close to Balfour. It gave wonderful service on that crossing until 1947, when it was replaced by what was to be the pride of the public works department ferry branch for many years, the MV *Anscomb*.

Before leaving sternwheelers, it should be noted that the government operated a sternwheeler as a ferry across the Fraser River from Ladner to Woodward's Landing for many years and, early in the 1900s, ran another on the same river from Quesnel to Prince George before finally building a river crossing and a usable road between these points.

The MV *Anscomb* was named after one of the most diligent ministers of public works that B.C. ever had. Herbert Anscomb served throughout most of the Second World War, and he had very few persons or dollars to work with, but he did very well anyway. His namesake ship was built in a shipyard in the Lower Mainland at a total cost of $393,000. The 170-foot-long ferry was then taken apart and reassembled in Nelson on the ancient sternwheeler ways, which were still in existence in 1947. These were equipped with windlasses, intended to be powered by teams of horses, to move the cradles up the ways. Fortunately the *Anscomb* was to go down the ways, not up them, but even so it got well and truly stuck when they tried to launch it. Several bulldozers got their tracks wet before it sped into the water.

The *Anscomb* went into service from new landing docks built for it, one at Balfour (across the West Arm from Procter) and another at Kootenay Bay, a few miles up the eastern lakeshore from Gray Creek, the previous landing.[4] It did very well for its first two years, but then it came under a cloud due to a remarkable lack of planning.

In 1949 it had completed two years of service, and according to federal government rules it had to be pulled out of the water for hull inspection. Appalled at the thought of using these troublesome ways once again, the ferry superintendent in Victoria stalled and stalled until finally, in 1951, he was told the vessel must either be inspected

The MV *Anscomb* was named after Herbert Anscomb, one of the most diligent ministers of public works the province ever had. The *Anscomb* was replaced by the *Osprey 2000* in the year 2000.

immediately or have its licence withdrawn. The superintendent promptly handed the problem over to the writer, the new district engineer at Nelson, and the ways were used. Horses were replaced by rubber-tired tractors, and the job was done.

All the cradles had to be totally rebuilt in the course of it. They came apart when the *Anscomb* was pulled out, and the ferry had to be jacked up while the work was done. This happened after the drive shafts to the propellers had been drawn, and local marine experts dolefully forecast that the hull would warp and the shafts would never go in again. With the use of multiple shims they were proven wrong.

A substitute ferry was required for several weeks during the refit, which included a scraping and repainting of the hull, and this led to the department using a sternwheeler once again as a ferry. In this case it was the SS *Moyie*, another CPR boat, and this was to be the provincial government's last use of these classic vessels.

Launched in 1898, the *Moyie* was loved by all until its demise in 1957. Its longevity, and that of its sister ship on the Arrow Lakes, the SS *Minto*, was due to the hulls being made of a composite of steel and wood, instead of being fully wooden.

The *Moyie*, accompanied by a steel car barge, was leased to the Department of Public Works by the CPR, and the captains of the *Anscomb* had to take command of it during the lease. This they did most admirably, especially considering that their skills were further tested by the requirement that the sternwheeler push a barge filled with motor vehicles. Their rather anxious drivers had to watch the operation from the deck of the sternwheeler. The grand old ship did the job wonderfully until the refurbished *Anscomb* returned to duty.

A great aid to the initial outstanding reliability of the *Anscomb* was its engines, which it used for the first 25 years of its life and which were of a quality seldom found today. The two six-cylinder

This classic photograph shows the SS *Moyie* pushing a huge rail transfer barge as a substitute ferry while the MV *Anscomb* was undergoing a refit. This took place between May 14 and 31 in 1951. As can be seen, it was necessary to put down a timber deck on the barge as otherwise automobiles and trucks would not have been able to move over the rails (the CPR forbade their removal). The steamer looks puny compared to the large steel barge, and when the strength of the current in the narrows at Balfour is considered, it's easy to realize the difficulty and skill required in handling this operation. It was achieved without mishap.

Vancouver-made Vivian diesels of 500 horsepower each gave wonderful service, and they did it silently and smoothly at very slow revolutions, in sharp contrast to their more modern noisy and vibration-prone replacements. These engines must have made close to 100,000 crossings of Kootenay Lake.

One thing different about them was the means of stopping and reversing them, and thereby stopping or reversing the rotation of the propeller shafts that were directly linked to the engines. This was done by spinning a wheel on the outside of each engine connected to the camshaft. (The reader will have to consult an automotive engineer to learn more about this!) This leads to the story of the oiler who got the port engine running full ahead instead of full astern in the turn eastbound out of Balfour one day, resulting in a noisy crash into some boathouses at Procter. This led in turn to a pregnant passenger giving birth immediately, with the oiler providing assistance, since he was the onboard first-aid man.

It was not unusual for *Anscomb* crew members, like the unfortunate oiler mentioned above, to extend a helping hand to travellers over the years, especially in the early days. A weak battery leading to a non-start on the ferry always brought assistance, there was always a crew member there to help with a tire change when a flat was discovered, and on one occasion a broken fan belt was replaced from a stock held on board. Traffic was much lighter then, of course, although with the improvement of the roads and the ferry services it increased steadily. Even though the SS *Nasookin* could theoretically carry 30 cars, it is reported that it never carried more than an average of six.

There is no record of the number of vehicles carried by the *Anscomb* in its first years, but it was stated that in the first period of service, from June 27, 1947, to March 31, 1948, it never missed a single trip, a wonderful testimonial to these engines. Later in the spring and summer of 1948, a flood totally submerged the road on the Creston Flats, and there was no through traffic moving at all between Nelson and Creston for more than a month.

There is one more story about the *Anscomb* and the *Moyie* that bears retelling, but in this case neither is substituting for the other. It seems that one day as the *Moyie* neared Kaslo on its regular run from Procter to Crawford Bay and then up the lake to Kaslo and Lardeau, it broke a drive shaft to its paddlewheel.[5] It drifted helplessly in the wind and current and finally ended up on the lakeshore somewhere between Crawford Bay and Riondel on the east side of the lake, a stranded vessel.

The crew did not have a radio—the CPR was not modernized enough for that—but they did have a telephone that they could attach to an overland telephone line. They connected it to the lakeside line running in to Riondel. By phone they put in a "call for assistance" to the federal department of transport. The department passed this on to the MV *Anscomb* by radio, and that vessel was bound by maritime custom to respond. The captain of the *Anscomb* immediately unloaded his passengers and vehicles at Balfour and, as the sun set, continued northwards to render assistance.

There was still enough light to see the beached sternwheeler when the *Anscomb* reached it. It was lying beyond the shallows, quite high on the beach, with its bow to the land and stern to the water. The crew had taken a mooring line ashore and attached it to a tree beside the telephone line they had used to make their call for assistance. Not expecting help until morning, they had doused the fire to their boiler and lost steam. They still had a wood stove to keep them warm.

The *Anscomb* could not come closer than 100 feet due to the shallow water, so the captain was glad that he had brought an extra tow line with him. He launched a lifeboat and took the line to them, then pulled them into deeper water and, with the help of the lifeboat crew, turned the sternwheeler around once it was fully afloat, put the line to its bow, transferred the line to the stern of the *Anscomb* and commenced the tow. Sad to say, everyone forgot about the line tied to the tree, and the tree came down on the telephone line. Riondel lost its connection to the world, but only temporarily. They cast off the tree as it followed them down the beach.

It was unfortunate that the *Moyie* did not have steam up, as the crew could not use their forward windlass to shorten the line, and the *Anscomb* had no such facility in its stern quarters, so the tow was on a 100-foot-long line. This posed problems for docking the derelict craft at Procter, but the senior captain of the *Anscomb* was up to the challenge. He stopped and turned his vessel off Procter, and letting the *Moyie* drift by on the current until at full line's length, he skillfully brought off, in the dark of night, what is called a slingshot landing, swinging his tow round on the end of its line and neatly bringing it in against its berth.

The *Moyie* berthed for the last time in April 1957. It is preserved at Kaslo after 59 very active years.

In 1972, after 25 years of service, the *Anscomb* was stripped to the car deck and completely rebuilt. Twelve years before that, the superstructure had been raised to give more clearance for trucks. Many people believe the character of the vessel was lost in the refit. Certainly it was vastly changed in the engine room, which was not fit to visit without ear protection due to the noise of the new high-speed engines.

In 1954, to provide additional service to meet the increased traffic on the route, the MV *Balfour* was put into service. It carries 36 cars and

The MV *Balfour* carries 36 cars and 150 passengers.

150 passengers. Now, every summer, American cars appear on board the *Balfour* and the *Osprey 2000* (which replaced the *Anscomb* in 2000). The inhabitants of the communities to the south enjoy the trip and its wonderful scenery, entirely without charge.

The problem of yearly inspection was solved by the construction of a floating dry dock, which was located at Sunshine Bay, west of Harrop. There is another floating dry dock moored at Southbank for the Francois Lake ferry. This ferry originally had a marine railway, which is an alternative solution to the problem of getting a ferry out of the water to inspect its hull. Such a railway was built on the landing ramp at Shelter Bay for the Galena Bay to Shelter Bay ferries crossing Upper Arrow Lake. The Arrow Lake ferries were first taken out for inspection on the old CPR sternwheeler ways at Nakusp.

The Galena Bay to Shelter Bay ferry route crosses the northern extremity of Upper Arrow Lake. In 1969 the ministry placed in service the MV *Galena*, which carries 35 cars and 200 passengers. A modern vessel, it is propelled by an innovative power system, manufactured in Germany. In each of the two corners at the after end of the hull there is a diesel-driven power unit. From this unit, a flat circular moving plate protrudes on the under side of the vessel, and vanes project downwards from the plate. Each vane moves on its own axis to produce motion in any direction. The vessel can literally rotate within its own length.

The MV *Galena*, which carries 35 cars and 200 passengers, went into service in 1969.

By using this power system, the branch demonstrated its readiness to accept new ideas, which in this case were fully successful. The only difficulty is the time taken to receive spare parts, something BC Ferries should think about in its present building program.

A companion vessel on the same route, the *Shelter Bay*, is similarly powered. The *Shelter Bay* was previously the *Needles* because it was located there. Its name changed when it moved after the return of a cable ferry, which took the "Needles" name.

This raises the issue of ferry names, and specifically the question of naming a ferry after a politician, something rather carefully avoided in recent years, although there were two named thus not too long ago, both at the coast. These were the *Westwood* and the *George S. Pearson* (a privately owned vessel that is described in more detail below), both names of politicians representing Nanaimo.[6] The *Anscomb* was not the first to be so burdened in the Interior, as it was preceded by a vessel named the *Rolf Bruhn*. This craft has an intriguing history. Built in Prince Rupert in sections, this six-car ferry was shipped by train to Burns Lake and then by road to Francois Lake, put together and launched and named, unimaginatively, the *Francois Lake Ferry*.

That was in 1922, and after 27 years of service it was replaced by a larger vessel capable of carrying 10 more cars. As they once again had

The MV *Omineca Princess* is shown here in dry dock, lifted out at the stern. It will be similarly lifted at the bow. Built on the coast, it was then shipped by rail and road to Francois Lake in pieces, then reassembled and launched in 1976 at a cost of $2.7 million. At 192 feet long with a 56-foot beam and weighing 765 gross tons, it operated throughout the severe winter of 1977–78 on a normal schedule, often in temperatures of -40°F. It never missed a trip, even in dense fog, when it often travelled without radar because the radar equipment belt drives repeatedly froze up. Its hull configuration proved operational in conditions of heavy slush and heavy ice floes. Parts of Francois Lake were covered by ice up to 28 inches thick that winter, but the vessel kept its channel clear. When it was tied up at night in winter, the dock surrounds were kept ice-free by a system of bubbling compressed air.

The *Omineca Princess*'s capacity for very large trucks and construction equipment proved very helpful during construction of the dam at Ootsa Lake, and is a continuing boon for the local logging industry and the economy.[7]

the original vessel in pieces, they lengthened it 10 feet and shipped it to Sicamous for service on Shuswap Lake. Here it replaced the ferry *G.B. Wright*, named after a historical figure rather than a political one, the renowned road builder of the mid-1800s, Gustavus Blin Wright.

When our itinerant "make and break" ferry was reassembled and modernized, it gained its final name, the *Rolf Bruhn*, and it made its first trip in these new waters in June 1952. Its namesake was a former public works superintendent who entered politics as a Conservative for the Salmon Arm riding, became minister of public works in 1929 and

The MV *G.B. Wright,* seen here carrying a full load of five cars, was named for renowed road builder Gustavus Blin Wright.

left that office in 1932. He was once again elected and appointed to the same position in 1941, again with the Conservatives, but he died in his first year in office.

The ferry named for him made its last trip on Shuswap Lake on April 13, 1956, when the service was terminated, but that was not the end of its career. It was once again taken apart and sent in pieces to Woodfibre at the head of Howe Sound, where it started service in salt water in May 1957, losing out to a larger boat in 1961. Now it could be moved to a new route under its own power and in one piece. It went to Nanaimo, where it substituted on the Gabriola route, and then was used

The MV *Rolf Bruhn*, built in Prince Rupert, has an intriguing history.

to help out at Hornby Island. Finally it was used as a substitute wherever needed until it was sold in 1977.

This craft put in 55 years of service, being assembled three times and torn apart twice. It was surpassed in the service life of its hull by the *Anscomb*, which in 2004 was badly treated after 57 years of service. Sold to a private party and moored at Ainsworth, it suffered a sinking, apparently caused by frost-broken water pipes.

As well as the services mentioned above, the coastal division of the highways department ferries branch ran many more ferry routes to otherwise inaccessible communities on B.C.'s multi-fractured coast, and also over the lower Fraser River at Ladner, Albion, Mission and Agassiz. The service at Ladner commenced in 1913, and three sternwheel ferries were used: the *W.H. Ladner*, the *Beaver* and the *Ladner-Woodwards No. 3*. After these came two propeller-driven vessels, the *Agassiz* and then the *Delta Princess*, which was renamed the *Saltspring Queen* and moved to serve Saltspring Island when the George Massey Tunnel opened in 1959.

Mention of Saltspring Island brings to mind an event there involving the *George S. Pearson*, another politician-named vessel. Its namesake represented Nanaimo for many years, and he also looked after the Gulf Islands. "Looked after" is a fitting term for George Pearson's governance when it came to public works on these islands. A reader of the public works road files collected during his tenure will note that he wrote at least twice a month to all the Gulf Island road foremen, individually detailing exactly what work they would do in the next two-week period. It was not surprising that they named a ferry after him. He was into everything.

In 1955, Saltspring Island's private ferry company, Gulf Island Ferry (founded 1951), decided to start another ferry service to Saltspring Island from Vancouver Island. The company was led by Gavin Mouat and was already running a service from Fulford to Swartz Bay. The new service would run from Crofton to Vesuvius Bay. Mouat had used his not inconsiderable influence to persuade the federal government to build docks at those two points, which he could use for his planned ferry route.

The opening ceremony was set for November 10, 1955, at the Crofton dock. Unfortunately, that was not a good day weatherwise, as there were gale-force winds, gale-lashed seas and blowing spray everywhere in Stuart Channel. Mouat was white-faced as he steadied the local beauty queen, who was almost blown over when she cut the ribbon at Crofton, but he was determined that the opening would go ahead. He had a huge luncheon meeting set up in Ganges to entertain the numerous dignitaries whom he had invited to this great occasion.[8] These included Lieutenant-Governor George S. Pearkes and Mrs. Pearkes, Victoria mayor Claude Harrison and Mrs. Harrison, and other ferry company officials and politicians.

The writer, who was district engineer for the highways ministry, was also present, and after the ferry had got underway and was halfway across the channel, he was in conversation with Captain Maude, the superintendent of the ferry company, standing on the foredeck, when both noticed that the wood-framed superstructure of the *George S. Pearson* was moving independently of its hull. This was no doubt due to the violent movement of the vessel as it progressed across the run of the five-foot waves. Just then this movement overturned a fire bucket on the deck house roof, and the sand in the bucket rained down on a woman standing with the mayor's wife. This woman promptly had hysterics.

The crew attempted to turn around and return to Crofton, which was much more sheltered than Vesuvius Bay, but that made things worse, and then a voice on the loudspeaker system asked Captain Maude to go to the bridge, where he took charge in the emergency. A forestry department tug, which Gavin Mouat had asked for to accompany the ferry across, turned around and went back to Crofton, leaving the old ferry to its fate.

Fortunately Captain Maude was equal to the challenge. He brought the ferry in as best it could be done at Vesuvius with a high following sea—sadly, this incurred quite serious damage to the new dock. People could disembark but not cars. It was several days before the mayor, or the district engineer, got their cars back. The luncheon went ahead, and northbound passengers returned to Crofton on the forestry tug, which by then had made it to Vesuvius Bay in lesser seas. The Queen's Own Rifles drum and bugle band played conscientiously all through the trip.

The *George S. Pearson* was formerly on ferry service in the United States under the name *Fox Island* before it was purchased by the Saltspring Island company. Their other vessel was the renowned *Cy Peck*.

It was a sad day when the coastal division of the highways ministry was transferred to the BC Ferry Corporation in 1985. At that time the Ministry of Transportation and Highways operated 32 major ferries on 36 routes. In 1991, after the removal of the coastal division, it served 16 routes with 11 major ferries, 6 reaction ferries and 2 subsidized ferries.

Before its day of reckoning came, the ferry branch acquired two large ferries, comparable in size to most of the vessels in the BC Ferry Corporation fleet. These were the *Sechelt Queen*, which was acquired from the corporation and went into service on the Comox to Powell River run in 1976, and the *Princess of Vancouver*, which was acquired from the CPR in 1982 and replaced the *Sechelt Queen*. This ferry was converted from side loading to bow loading.

In contrast to the *Sechelt Queen*—which was 4,979 gross tons, had 6,560-horsepower engines and could carry 475 passengers and 83 cars—one should consider the first ferry on the coast run by the government. The *Catherine Graham* was 65 gross tons, had 110 horsepower and carried 8 cars and about 45 passengers. It ran between Buckley Bay and Denman Island for nearly 20 years, making its last run in February 1973. It was replaced by a ferry of 28-car capacity. The *Catherine Graham* was the first

The MV *George S. Pearson* was named for a Nanaimo politician.

The MV *Princess of Vancouver* was purchased from the CPR in 1982 and converted to a bow-loading ferry for the Comox-to-Powell River run. It was the largest vessel in the Ministry of Highways fleet, capable of carrying 170 cars. Its bow aprons probably reduced its 18-knot speed.

government-owned ferry on the coast. There, as elsewhere, the operators of subsidized ferries continually asked for larger subsidies and seldom added capacity soon enough to ensure good service. That was why they disappeared in favour of the better-run government service. The *Catherine Graham* replaced the barge pulled by the tug *Billy B*, which replaced the passenger launch *Moniker*, which replaced the tug *Garry Point* with scow, which started the service in August 1930.

The Ministry of Highways coastal ferry division ran smoothly for many years. It had no labour problems, it did not build the wrong kind of ferries, it suited the job it did and it fully fitted the truism "If it ain't broke, don't fix it." More lucid reasoning would have limited BC Ferries' increase of its coastal empire to the Comox–Powell River run and nothing more, as it would be much more efficient for the present Ministry of Transportation to run short-distance ferry routes to small islands or remote communities.

The MV *Catherine Graham*, an eight-car ferry that served the Buckley Bay-to-Denman Island run from 1954 to 1973, it was named for a girl born on a previous ferry on this run, the MV *Moniker*.

The road and ferry crews become significant parts of such communities and their political-complaint-solving processes and for this reason it would have been much better if the ferries had remained under direct provincial government control.[9]

With the advent of the Gordon Campbell Liberal government, privatization of the interior ferries commenced in September 2003. We can only hope that the new privateers of the Interior do better than their very early predecessors.

Up In the Air Too

No account of the conveyances operated by the provincial government to ferry people around the province would be complete without mention of the Government Air Service, which for most of its life consisted of the Air Services Branch—first of the Department of Public Works (DPW), and later of the Ministry of Highways.

Around the mid-20th century, the DPW acquired an aircraft and a pilot. The plane, a twin-engined wartime Anson, served without mishap through the 1950s, mostly moving personnel between Victoria and Vancouver. Its lack of a pressurized cabin inhibited its use for crossing B.C.'s mountains, but not too much. Sadly, it lost power in one engine on takeoff from Pat Bay Airport in 1962 and crashed; two people died.

In the early 1960s, the government bought four Beechcraft 18 twin-engined planes. One was assigned to the Department of Lands for air photography, and the others went to the highways department. They were also successful, but soon became outdated when turboprop engines came into fashion. The Air Services Branch then rebuilt one Beechcraft 18 in its hangar at Pat Bay, installing turboprop engines and converting from a tail wheel to a nose wheel undercarriage. Named *Southwind*, this plane became a real workhorse.

The advent of pressurization led to the purchase of newer planes, including two Beechcraft A200s and the most successful plane of them all, the Cessna Citation 500, with two jet engines. It was supplemented by a larger Cessna Citation II, used primarily for air ambulance work, as were the other Citations. In 1979 the service ran four round-trip flights daily from Victoria to Vancouver, and it flew province-wide as required. It carried 13,070 passengers and made 553 ambulance flights. The branch's 1984 annual report shows ambulance flights almost doubled and passenger load almost halved.[10]

The ministry lost the branch in the late 1980s, and in 1994 the people lost it to privatization. This followed the acquisition of five Citation jets and a Canadair Challenger, an excellent long-range business jet that was bought against the advice of the branch director. Premier Bill Vander Zalm wanted an aircraft that could fly him nonstop to Ottawa. It was more airplane than the branch could really use, and it overtaxed the hangar capacity. This and other factors convinced Premier Mike Harcourt he had no alternative but to dissolve the branch, a decision he later regretted. Sadly, these excellent aircraft were sold for much less than their true value.

A Cessna Citation ambulance plane of the Air Services Branch in 1979.

CHAPTER 6

THE TREK OF THE HUSCROFTS IN 1891

The story of a pioneer family's journey from the Green River in Utah to the Kootenay River in British Columbia. The paterfamilias simply wanted his own land, untrammelled and basically uncontrolled.

*T*his is the story of two emigrants from England to the Utah Territory of the United States, who met in their new country and married and then immigrated again, this time to British Columbia, Canada. On this second migration, they were accompanied by 8 of their 10 surviving children. That the last move of this transportation drama was accomplished by horse and wagon, travelling over 900 miles through largely unmapped, unpopulated and quite mountainous countryside, and that one part of the journey involved a roughly made raft on a tortuous river, may give the reader some idea of the adventures involved. But to tell this story fully it is necessary to go into the causes as well as the results. Why did William Rodger Huscroft and Jane Fisher leave England in the first place? Why did they leave Utah for British Columbia in the second place?

There were two reasons they left Utah. One will become evident as the events of their stay there unfold. The other was simply a dream of a green and temperate paradise, so tempting when one lives in the harsh sun-drenched desert of the Great Salt Lake valley. In the last decade of the 19th century, this dream came to William Rodger Huscroft when he was 61 years of age.

The verdant valley he sought was that of the Kootenay River in British Columbia, a developing province in Canada. More specifically, his dream was of that part of the river where it flows back into Canada immediately before it widens into Kootenay Lake, a section then known as the Kootenay Flats.

William and Jane Huscroft arrived in that valley in 1891. They were the first non-Native family to settle there.[1] Their impact was substantial because it planted the seed of permanence in an area which previously was frequented by a transitory population, mostly composed of miners and prospectors, and where the Native culture had been decimated by the newcomers' diseases.

The First Adventure—England to the United States, 1851–60

William Huscroft and Jane Fisher left England for the same reason that many good people crossed the Atlantic Ocean to come to the New World in the 19th century: the Industrial Revolution. This source of upheaval, with its dreadful effects on health and living conditions in Britain, changed the way of life of many people and was accentuated by a class system that unfairly limited land ownership in that country. Little further needs to be said of this here, but it does affect many of William's and Jane's decisions.

The underlying motivation to move, and the cause of their uprooting from both Britain and the United States, was the Church of Jesus Christ of Latter-day Saints, otherwise known as the Mormon Church, founded by Joseph Smith in 1830 in New York State. How these people and this church got together in these days needs explanation. In some ways it is sad, and in other ways inspiring.[2]

Missionaries from this new religious order, which considered itself a communion of saints, had spread the word in Britain between 1837 and 1845, baptizing converts as they went. In the latter part of that period they were led by Brigham Young, one of the Twelve Apostles of the church. Their mission was to recruit members in Britain who would emigrate to the United States to help them overcome the strong opposition building up against the church there. One example of this opposition was the Haun's Hill Massacre in Missouri in 1838, where a detachment of the state militia swooped down on an outlying Mormon

The Industrial Revolution and What It Meant

The Industrial Revolution in Britain occurred between 1750 and 1830, but its effects lasted much longer. Prior to the "revolution," an agricultural reorganization had taken place in the country. It started with the destruction of the common-field system, which allowed tenant farmers to add to their rented acreage by the free use of common land. This severe blow to the small farmer was followed by the Enclosure movement, in which common property and waste lands were "enclosed" in private ownership. This move to much larger farms (consolidation of farms was as much as 20 to 1) wiped out marginal tenant farmers at the same time as it increased efficiency through measures such as crop rotation. This in turn led to large numbers of agricultural workers being unemployed.

This rural upheaval coincided with the growth of factories, which used such technological advances as the steam engine, the power loom, and iron forging and fabrication. Towns and cities sprang up around burgeoning workplaces, mostly in the north of England and lowland Scotland. Displaced farmers and agricultural workers concentrated there, as well as throngs of Irish immigrants seeking work, which led to huge increases in the numbers of town dwellers. Leeds, for example, doubled in population between 1801 and 1830. Lancashire saw an 80 percent increase in 20 years within the same period.

Contributing to the Irish migration was the death of 2 million Irish in the Great Famine, caused in large part by the stubbornness, stupidity and almost total lack of human compassion in both Houses of Parliament in London. It was no wonder that hungry thousands flocked across the Irish Sea to the industrial cities of Britain—to the great benefit of their oppressors.

The worst shame of the period was child labour. Thousands of pauper children, from five years in age, worked 14-hour days. Their elders were not much better off. In 1799 the Combination Act decreed that as few as two men getting together to discuss improving their lot at work faced imprisonment for up to three months—and all this while the cotton industry tripled in size!

Another irony was that town dwellers learned how to create the metal pipes that would bring water from nearby rivers, and they learned to make the bricks and tiles for sewers to send their filth to these streams, but they did not know to keep them apart, and contaminated drinking water brought cholera.

Despite its excesses, the Industrial Revolution was hugely successful economically. By 1850 Britain was producing two-thirds of the world's coal, half its iron and half its commercial cotton. However, dreadful living conditions brought dreadful disease. Wealth for some brought no well-being for others. It was little wonder that William Huscroft and many more wished to leave.[3]

settlement, killing 17 people and wounding many more. The militia acted on orders from Governor L.W. Boggs, who insisted that "the Mormons must be exterminated or driven from the State." (One reason for the drastic opposition to this new Christian religious community, aside from a human response to those who consider themselves special, was thought to be the Mormons' rejection of slavery.)

It was only the remarkable immigration into Missouri and nearby states of Mormons from Britain that saved the church in these years. The next step was the trek across to Utah following the discovery of Great Salt Lake in 1847 by an emissary of Brigham Young. The lake was designated the promised land.

This brings us to our subject family. The dirt and degradation the Industrial Revolution brought to British cities and towns (not to mention the cholera epidemics of the 1840s through the 1860s) certainly contributed to the exodus from the British Isles, as did religious conviction, but it was the hope of owning land that loomed largest. This was certainly a motivating factor for William Rodger Huscroft, a native of Somerton, Yorkshire, England. He was born there in 1830, reportedly an orphan soon thereafter, and he left England in 1851 on the ship *Ellen*, having joined the Mormon Church in 1850.

Emma and John Fisher joined the Mormons in 1849, the year before Huscroft did. Their daughter Jane was too young to join then; she was baptised later. The Fisher family left England for America four years after that, departing on a sailing ship named the *International* on February 25, 1853, in company with 422 other Mormons. The passenger list also contained a future American president, Chester A. Arthur. The 5,000-mile trip was supposed to take five to six weeks, but after eight weeks of sailing, on April 23, they finally docked in New Orleans, Louisiana. Nearly everyone left the ship there because almost every person on board who was not already a member was baptized into the Church of Latter-day Saints during the ocean voyage—including the crew. The only exceptions were the steward and his wife (staunch Catholics), the third mate (who was evidently of no religion and was described as an evil man) and of course Chester Arthur (he became president when John Garfield was assassinated in 1881). On the trip there were 7 births, 7 deaths, 5 marriages and 47 baptisms.

From New Orleans they transferred to a riverboat and steamed up the Mississippi River past Louisiana, Arkansas and Missouri to Iowa. These states, along with Minnesota, were the western boundary of civilization in the United States at that period, with outposts in California and Texas.

After leaving the river at Keokuk, Iowa, at the eastern border of the state, the group went overland to Council Bluffs on Iowa's western boundary, the starting point for the trip through the wilderness to the Utah Territory, which was then largely under the control of Brigham Young. Their destination was Provo, Utah, located on the east shore of Utah Lake, about 40 miles south of Salt Lake City.

In Council Bluffs they came under the care of The Perpetual Emigration Company (they had a way with names in these years), which had been organized to look after them. Forty covered wagons were made available to those who could afford to pay. The Fishers could, so they rode; others could not, so they walked and pushed handcarts with their belongings on the 1,000-mile trip to Great Salt Lake. During this trip they encountered an enterprising young man operating a raft across a river as a ferry. The young ferryman took a liking to one family's daughter, and she to him, and they were married on the spot by the captain of the wagon train. The daughter stayed with him, but years later this couple, quite well to do and with a growing family, arrived in Provo and the girl was reunited with her family.

The Fishers settled in Provo, Utah, in 1853, and in 1868 Emma became a teacher with the Relief Society of the Church, where she worked for many years. Jane's brothers, James and George, were born in Utah. James married and had five children.

Soon after they arrived in Utah, the Fishers met William Rodger Huscroft. Huscroft was described as powerfully built, strong, stern, independent, solemn and determined. The impression gained from his photograph is of a square and sturdy man. With this nature and demeanour it is little wonder that he soon chafed under a church leader who was quite dictatorial. Not much is known of his trip or of his first years in America, but it is known that he did not subscribe to the practice of polygamy, so dear to the heart of his religious and secular leader, Brigham Young. (When Young died in 1877, he was survived by

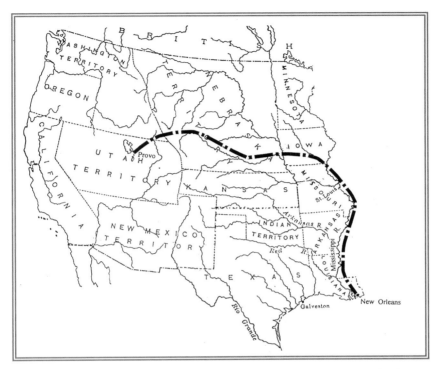

The Western Half of the United States in the Mid-1800s: Shown here is the route taken by Jane Fisher and her parents in their journey from New Orleans to Provo in Utah Territory.

The American West was generally considered to be west of the Mississippi River and west of the western boundaries of Minnesota., Iowa, Missouri, Arkansas and Louisiana. Within this area, only Texas, California and Oregon were states as we know them now.

Jane Fisher and her parents arrived in New Orleans by sailing ship in late April 1853. They went up the Mississippi by riverboat to Keokuk, Iowa, by land to Council Bluffs, Iowa, and then in a 40-wagon train to Provo, arriving there in the late autumn. The journey was 1,200 miles by land and 800 miles by river—2,000 miles in all.

17 wives and 47 children.) Huscroft had already resisted that temptation for two years when Jane Fisher arrived in Utah in 1853, but after he met her he soon succumbed to espousal, on the singular basis, and they were married in Provo on July 23, 1856, when Jane was 15 years old. He took no further wives.

This was undoubtedly the best way for him, because Jane, a woman of spirit, intelligence and tenacity, wholeheartedly joined with him in dismissing the practice of polygamy. She was supported in this by her mother and by her grandmother, who remained in England.

Understandably this did not endear them to the ruling Mormons, although it is recorded that William dedicated all his worldly possessions to the church as was their custom—although this may well have been involuntary. In any case, the Huscrofts settled down in Utah, where the new husband took up his old-country trade of harness making, including the making of shoes and whips. (His son John, in later years, said that his father never seemed to have any desire to learn new trades, being particularly inept with an axe and with guns, in which John was expert. A gunman or not, the son said the father never lacked in courage.)

The Second Adventure—Provo to Missouri and Back, 1860–91

William and Jane's married life took the usual course, in these pioneer years, of regular childbirth, but it was spread out over a somewhat more extended time than usual. Emma Jane was born in 1860, William Rodger in 1862, Mary Elizabeth in 1864 and George Joseph in March 1867 in Provo. More children came later, but at that time the course of their lives took an abrupt turn because they picked up what they could carry and suddenly left Utah, retracing their steps back down the Oregon Trail in the wrong direction to the start of the trail in Independence, Missouri. It is reported they settled near there, at or around Birmingham, Missouri.

Why this happened and, in fact, exactly when it happened remain, to a great extent, a mystery in the family's history, surrounded by rumour but not much fact. One version of the family history says that this move occurred in 1860, another that it was in 1863. The latter date was the year the Reorganized Church of Mormon campaigned for members in Utah, and William and Jane may have joined it then because it was against polygamy. This was a time of turmoil and division in the church and in the country, as it was embroiled in civil war, and, among other things, the Mormons were accused of favouring the Confederacy—which was a switch because originally they had been persecuted for rejecting slavery!

A third version of the family history says that William and Jane went east in 1867. This last account would have had them leave when George Joseph was only a few weeks old, but it has the advantage of being after the Civil War. The other scenarios, which have them protected by the army in 1863 or running, unprotected, from the vengeance of Brigham

Young's goons (known as the Avenging Angels) in 1860, are much more colourful, but less credible. In any event, their next offspring, James Frederick and Anne Effie, were reported as being born in Missouri in 1869 and 1872 respectively.

Jane's mother and father did not accompany them; they remained true to the original church. The wrench to Jane of leaving her parents and returning to the discomfort of trail travel with her children can barely be imagined, and since they lost all their possessions that they could not carry, there must have been a profound reason for their departure.

The period when they were first in Utah (1853 and onward), living near Provo, was a time of great stress between the Mormons and other American immigrants to the west. In 1857 the worst incident, the Mountain Meadows Massacre, occurred. The Fancher Train, a wagon train of non-Mormons, came through Provo heading south, and the residents of Provo were told not to give the travellers any food or aid. When the Fancher Train was about 170 miles away from Provo, a group of Mormons, said to be from a settlement named Cedar City, ambushed it. Of the 120 men, women and children in the train, only 17 children were spared.[4]

The attack was said to be revenge for the killing of Joseph Smith in Illinois 27 years earlier. The Fancher group contained emigrants from Illinois, and the Mormons had informants there to identify their former enemies. The result was that the American army moved into the area. This was the start of the short-lived Mormon War and the difficulty with the federal government that came with it, all brought to a standoff by the Civil War as much as by anything else. President James Buchanan swore he would replace Brigham Young, but he never did.

It later came out that some residents of Provo, including William Huscroft, had been kind to members of the Fancher Train, and this may have been an early reason for his alienation from the church. Another story is that Brigham Young ordered Huscroft to join the avenging group and he refused, and that is why he left to go east.

William Huscroft must have been aware of the Saints' harassment, intimidation and exploitation of the Gentiles passing through the Salt Lake valley on their way to California in the early 1850s. Not only did they overcharge for supplies and for the use of their ferries, but they also occasionally levied tolls for the use of the trail in the valley, and sometimes they closed it entirely, forcing wagon trains to break trail through the desert.

Then there was the ruse of delaying trains arriving late in the season so that they missed the last date of departure for safe passage through the Sierras. These latecomers had to stay over in the valley and became "winter Mormons." The conspiracy continued with merchants charging high costs for everything the travellers needed, forcing them to become very cheap labour for the Saints' building programs in Salt Lake City in order to make ends meet. Certainly this would not sit well with any fair-minded man.

William might also have been disillusioned religiously. A minister from another Protestant church attended one of Brigham Young's church services around that time. He reported that "Young preached Joseph Smith rather than Jesus Christ, Mormonism rather than Christianity." This theory is given some weight by the fact that William was baptized into the Reorganized Mormon Church in 1865.

Those who adhere to the Mormon faith may agree that Brigham Young was a complete dictator, but they dispute suggestions that he was anything other than a benevolent one. They particularly question the final theory put forward in the family history to explain why William and Jane left Utah. This was that Brigham Young, the father of 47 children, was not always particular about who served him in this procreation of the faith, and he would occasionally choose wives of others in his flock. He was reputed to be particularly in favour of young women with small children. In the mid-1860s, Jane Huscroft fell into this category. William Huscroft, it is surmised, heard that Jane was on the list, and that is why he left so hurriedly. It certainly was a reason that would justify the drastic action he took.

Pertaining to this, Mick Huscroft's recollections of discussions with his father are of interest. Mick is the name by which John Huscroft's fourth son, Donald William, is known, and in the family history he wrote: "Men who by whatever means reach a position of absolute power, will abuse it. Indeed, those in this position who do not abuse it are the exceptional ones. Behaviour of this kind is often hidden by religion, if, indeed, absolute power ever needs an excuse."[5]

Viewed in a harsh, irreligious light over 120 years after the fact, Brigham Young's achievements were astonishing. He went to another country; recruited thousands of individuals and families to his religious sect; arranged for their transportation, at their cost, over the ocean; and settled them in his country in direct defiance of at least two state governors there. Then, when he realized that there was no future for him in the east, he found a promised land in the ungoverned wilderness of the west. He organized transportation for 1,000 miles of travel over land, right down to the vehicles and roadway used, again at the travellers' cost. Finally, he set up one of history's best colonization projects at the chosen destination. There is no doubt that he could have been forgiven to a great extent for the dictatorship that was necessary for such an accomplishment—what posterity condemns him for is simply that he took too many wives.

More questions surround William and Jane's next move. Why did they leave Missouri for another 1,000-mile trek, back to Utah, less than a decade after their flight from Provo? One cause might have been the flooding by the Missouri River, an event to be expected as Birmingham is close to the river and extensive dyking was unknown then. Another could have been a hog cholera outbreak, which killed all their animals in that period, or it might simply have been Jane's natural desire to see her parents and to live near them now that time had passed and the opening of the Union Pacific transcontinental railway in 1869 had brought more order out west. Or was it because they heard that the "Utah bull" (Brigham Young) had lessened in vigour? (He died in 1877.) Likely a combination of the above.[6]

Details of their trip back to Utah from Missouri are as indistinct as those of their trip eastward six or more years before. They presumably travelled by covered wagon on the Oregon Trail through South Pass and down to the crossing of the Green River, immediately west of the continental divide in the present-day state of Wyoming (then Wyoming Territory). Here they probably left the historic trail and followed that river downstream for 100 miles into Utah Territory and on down to where the town of Jensen, Utah, stands today. They had a farm there, and their place of residence has been referred to as "Green River" and also, much later, as "Sandy" by John Huscroft (William and Jane's fourth son). This makes sense as they followed Big Sandy Creek to the new location.

Big Sandy Creek is a tributary of the Green River and originates close to South Pass. (Some of this is shown on the map on p. 148.)

The exact date they left Missouri remains in doubt, but they were back west when Sophy Mellissa was born in 1874. Her birth is recorded as taking place in Jensen, barely 20 miles inside the territorial boundary.

Why did they settle here? The geography of this part of Utah may provide a clue. As mentioned, entry from the east was by South Pass, which crosses the continental divide within the Rocky Mountains in Wyoming Territory at an elevation of 7,550 feet above sea level. This pass contained the combined Oregon, California and Mormon Trails. All three trails crossed the Green River about 53 miles farther on. Some 50 miles beyond that river crossing lay Fort Bridger, named for Jim Bridger, the mountain man, guide and trader who established it in 1843, four years before the Mormons first arrived. This is where the original Oregon trail struck off west and north to Fort Hall. Later, the Sublette Cutoff bypassed Fort Bridger, going directly from South Pass to Fort Hall. During a period between the 1840s and the 1860s, the Mormons operated ferries across the Green River on both the Sublette Cutoff and the main Oregon Trail, charging non-Mormons excessively for the use of them—up to $16 per wagon at times, but usually $3 to $5.

The trail on to Salt Lake City from Fort Bridger (a journey of approximately 85 miles) ran through Golden Pass, a divide in the Wasatch Range. However, if instead of proceeding to Golden Pass and Salt Lake City you followed the Green River, which flows almost due south, a trek of about 130 miles took you to Jensen, located on the west side of the river. (At one time there was also a ferry crossing the Green River here. The town was named after the family that first ran the ferry.) Between the crossing of the main trail and Jensen, the Green River flows through three huge canyons—the river's erosion there resembles that of the Colorado on a smaller scale—as it passes through another mountain range lying east to west, the Uinta Mountains, with the Uinta Basin immediately south of them. This basin stretches westward to the southern end of the Wasatch Range, and both ranges peter out beside the Provo River, which flows down to Provo, beside Utah Lake.

By the late 1860s the Mormons had brought water to every irrigable valley on either side of the Wasatch, following Brigham Young's edict that there would be no private ownership of any streams. The small greened-up area around Jensen was about the only irrigated land outside the larger Wasatch area, and this may well have been the reason William Huscroft settled there when he returned from Missouri, because it was separated from the Mormon centre, and Brigham Young, in Salt Lake City. Its location also made it easy to visit Provo, where Jane Huscroft's mother and father still lived, without going near Salt Lake City.

The Fishers were well-established, with a large home where the Huscroft children could stay while attending Provo Academy. Jane also went there for most of the births of her continuing maternity. John Henry and Maud Isabel were born in Jensen, while Sarah Etta and Charles Leroy were born in Provo. The final count was 11. One son, William Rodger (Jr.), died in 1872, when he was 11 years old, from a snake bite.

The family records, reported by a Fisher granddaughter, describe Jane's mother, Emma Burrows Fisher, as "tall, slim, with dark hair—a fashion plate—[she] always had beautiful clothes and [was] very aristocratic." She says that her aunt "Jane, too, was a very attractive woman. She had dark wavy hair, and like her mother was tall, slim, and stylish. She was always good natured, and she was an expert seamstress and a good cook. Her daughters were all attractive capable women too."[7]

The Third Adventure—The Trek from the Green River Valley in Utah Territory to the Kootenay River Valley in British Columbia in 1891

It might have been reasonable to think that after she delivered her last child in 1886, Jane would have wanted to relax and stay reasonably close to her mother for a while (her father had died in 1882). Jane had been steadily giving birth for 26 years, from age 19 to 45, producing five boys and six girls, and having been in one place for 10 years, she might have hoped that the wandering life was behind her. But this was not to be, because five years later, in 1891, when he was 61 years of age, William Rodger Huscroft got itchy feet and once more took to the trail in covered wagons. This time he headed for Canada, and he took all of his immediate family with him, except for Mary and George.

Two things might have influenced him. He provided a clue to the first a number of years later in Canada when he remarked, "Things are getting a bit crowded here, and it is maybe time that we moved on to Australia." William, it seemed, just wanted the unspoiled wilderness without too many people, and when that thought came to him in 1891 in Utah, nirvana was up north in British Columbia. It may have been a similar thought that brought him back to Utah from Birmingham, Missouri, 15 years earlier.

A second enticement for him to move out of Utah might have been the glowing accounts of the Kootenay valley, which must have seemed like a paradise to Americans moving north. William may have read a brochure produced by William Adolf Baillie-Grohman, a British sportsman, capitalist and aristocrat who was attempting to reclaim the rich land of the Kootenay Flats by diverting and dyking the Kootenay River. The word that got back south was that "the grass was as high as a horse's withers." (For the uninitiated, a horse's withers are the junction of the shoulder bones of a horse, the highest point of its back.) That grass was tall.

William Huscroft's decision to move may also have been triggered by the drawbacks of life with the Mormons, such as the regimentation, the

The Huscrofts came to Canada in wagons like these.

He Joined the Waters ... Temporarily

In the 1880s a British visitor, William Adolph Baillie-Grohman, undertook a perfectly feasible scheme to divert water from the upper Kootenay River into the Columbia River where the Kootenay, about 50 miles along its course, came close to the Columbia headwaters.[8] He believed this diversion would reduce the maximum flow of the Kootenay through the flats at the head of Kootenay Lake enough that he would be able to reclaim a huge area of that rich alluvial plain and protect it from annual flooding with a minimum of dyking.

By 1887 Baillie-Grohman had built a canal between the rivers at a place called Canal Flats, near Columbia Lake. He put out a brochure, widely circulated in nearby American states including the Utah Territory, in which he praised the wonderful Kootenay Flats. It is thought that William Huscroft might have seen a copy of this brochure. Three years before that, Baillie-Grohman had brought in the SS *Midge*, which was launched to serve the dyking project on the Kootenay.[9]

Baillie-Grohman's ingenious project was finally scuttled by the Dominion government, which controlled international rivers. The government was urged on by the CPR board of directors, which was concerned about the diversion's potential effect on their track. Without flood prevention, a much lesser acreage than originally intended was reclaimed at Creston.[10]

When the Huscrofts arrived in 1892, Baillie-Grohman's project was over, and he was gone. He had worked for nine years on it, reportedly crossing the Atlantic 30 times in pursuit of his dream, and squandering his fortune. Despite this, he never lost his respect for B.C. and the potential it had.

It is ironic that his dream was demolished by the railway he had regularly patronized. Grohman Creek near Nelson and Mount Grohman above it in the Selkirk Range are all he had to show for his efforts in the end. This photo shows him in his study in Europe.

restraints on water and land ownership, and the management of water and land. He and his family seem to have done well in Jensen, but despite this, and despite being over 60 years of age, Huscroft decided to pull up stakes and move north, to live under the Union Jack and to enjoy the benevolence of the Kootenay Flats. William and Jane planned their migration at their home by the Green River in Utah, and it is there that we join them.

Before starting the trip, they decided on the makeup of the party. Emma, their eldest child, was married to John Arrowsmith, and in 1891 they had four children—two daughters, eight and four years old; two sons, two and six years of age—and a baby on the way. The Arrowsmiths travelled north with the Huscrofts, but not all the way initially, as will be made clear later in the chapter.

Mary Elizabeth, William and Jane's second daughter, stayed on in Utah and married there. She died of cancer in 1896, and she never saw her parents again after they left. Jane's mother, Emma Burrows Fisher, also stayed on in Provo. She died there in 1905.

George Joseph, the eldest surviving boy, was 24 in 1891. He also remained in Utah, and the next year he married an Irish girl named Mary McKinney. They very soon followed in his parents' footsteps, and their first child, Vera Marie, was born in Bonners Ferry in 1893 while they were on their way north.

The remaining Huscroft offspring (unmarried) were three boys and four girls—James, 22; John, 13; Charles, 9; Effie, 19; Sophy, 15; Sarah, 11; and Maud, 5. To carry this company, as well as the two parents and all their worldly possessions, they decided on two heavy wagons and one light one for the Huscrofts, and one heavy wagon for the Arrowsmith parents and their four young children.

Therefore, when they left Jensen on the Green River in May 1891, there were three heavy wagons and one light wagon (which each required teams of two or four horses), a total of 50 horses and "twenty or more head of cattle." Quite a train! Their son James must be given the credit for this livestock coming with them. He had earned the money to purchase them by herding cattle in Wyoming in the months before. His herding experience would be well used on the trip.[11]

William Rodger, the father, would have driven one of the heavy wagons; James, the eldest son, another; and John Arrowsmith, the third.

The light wagon would have been driven either by son John or by one of the elder girls, Effie or Sophy. Driving the herd of spare horses and 20 or more cattle were two young men, names never mentioned, whom they took with them from Jensen. They might have been assisted by John from time to time, and even by one or more of the girls. Charles was too young for any responsibility, but could help out. The two men from Jensen left them at Kalispell to take work on the railway. By then they were close enough to their goal to handle the horses and cattle without them.

The travellers reportedly visited Provo on their way north for a last visit with Jane's mother. It is also said that they went through Wyoming, so they probably went back up the old trail to Fort Bridger and then by the old Oregon Trail north. It is ironic that they thereby passed through two remnants of pre-Mormon life in the area. These were Fort Hall and Fort Bridger, trading posts serving the original immigrants to Oregon and California. The first was founded by the Hudson's Bay Company, and the other by Jim Bridger, legendary mountain man, fur trader and guide.

Starting in 1843, Bridger constructed a remarkably successful emporium of log buildings. However, in the early 1850s the Mormons squeezed him out, ensuring his demise by bringing a lawsuit against him before a Mormon judge in a Mormon court, a favourite device of theirs. They accused him of selling stolen goods. The Saints finally burned most of Fort Bridger late in 1857 after they heard that a punitive expedition of the U.S. army was on its way west as a result of problems between the Mormons and California-bound emigrants. They feared that the soldiers would use Fort Bridger as a fortress. They built their own trading post beside it, calling it Fort Supply. It was events such as this that led William Huscroft to long for life under the British flag.

Beyond Fort Hall they probably first followed roads built by the Mormons, and then they would have come upon a number of roads built in the Montana mining boom of the 1880s. They saw the lights and heard the nighttime noises of Missoula, Montana, as they passed, but they did not call in—it was a wild town. Beyond Missoula the family left the mining road network and struck off northward through the huge Flathead Indian Reserve, often, as John says, rolling along through the sagebrush without the benefit of a road.[12] They then travelled along the east shore of Flathead Lake and from there north to Kalispell, Montana,

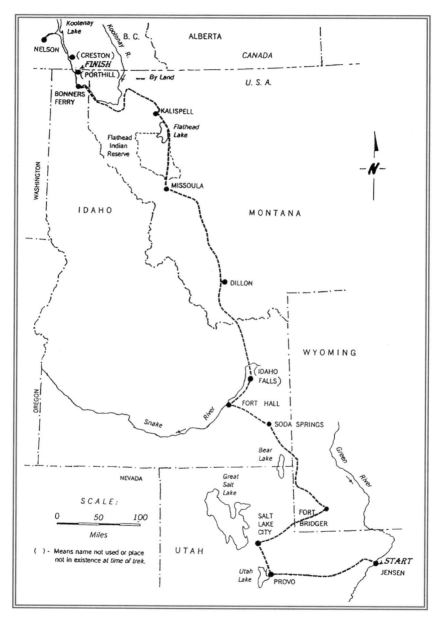

The trek of the Huscrofts in 1891

where they stopped and paused for a while. John Arrowsmith and his family stayed in that outpost for the winter.

But the Huscrofts did not, and after a reconnaissance ahead by William and John, they hit the road again. Fifteen miles north of Kalispell they met their third railway—they had already crossed the Union Pacific and the Northern Pacific. This one, the Great Northern, was under construction at the time, with the grade complete but no tracks, and mostly without bridges. It would be opened for its full length two years later. Here the rains came, and as they progressed along the muddy railway grade and struggled laboriously down and up again in the valleys, crossing the creeks for which there were no bridges, they did some damage to the fills and slopes. Finally, after they had covered nearly 100 miles of this, the contractors stopped them and said, "Go no further."

After some negotiation, the railwaymen relented and consented to a compromise: the women and children in the light wagon would proceed overland, but the heavier vehicles, with the great majority of their possessions, would not. James would pilot the women and girls, and Charles would go along with them. John, the 13-year-old, would remain with his father to assist him when they found a solution to their dilemma.

William questioned the contractors and determined that they had progressed far enough at that point to be past the Kootenay Falls, the main interruption to navigation on the loop of that river within the United States. There were some rapids between them and Bonners Ferry, but they were not too bad (or so the railwaymen said), and, best of all, William wanted to travel in the direction the current was flowing.

William and John got the idea of building a raft as a means of conveying the two larger wagons down the river (all the horses and the cattle would go with the overland party), and they set to work, felling trees and trimming logs by the river. Soon they had a raft built, 14 feet wide by 40 feet long, just large enough to carry the two big wagons (John Arrowsmith had kept one in Kalispell). All working together, they dismantled the wagons and loaded all parts of them and their contents aboard the raft.

At this point, just before William and 13-year-old John set off down the river, and just before the others left to travel along the grade to

Bonners Ferry in the light wagon, they had a change of plans. Along the right-of-way came a young man with a packsack, one of the multitude of wanderers tramping through the bush in those years. When he learned their destination, he asked for a ride, and William took him up immediately and promptly demoted son John to the wagon, a safer means of travel. William and his new helper pushed off, and the others also got underway.

According to John's memoirs, the raft party was going 15 miles an hour down the Kootenay River when he last saw them, and he could only wish them luck. The land party went on its way—but after travelling about a mile, John was surprised to see a figure standing on the cleared right-of-way ahead of them, a person who looked very much like his dad. It was William, and when they reached him, he told the story. The ride had been rough, they hit boulders constantly, and when the captain of the craft finally steered it to the shore, the mate, who was the sole crew member, mutinied and left without a word. The drifter had had enough, and he was gone! John was immediately reinstalled as mate, and all started again.

John says that it did not get better, only worse. Ahead of them they saw a canyon, a sheer cliff with a sharp turn of the stream before it, and a whirlpool. The raft struck the rock, tilted and almost sank. With the stern four feet under water, John, who was at the rear, climbed up on the stacked wagon wheels. The raft spun, righted itself and resumed its trip down the river, back to front. John was now the pilot, and somehow, with him using the rough paddle that they had made from a tree branch, they carried on to Bonners Ferry.

At Bonners Ferry the others joined the raft, and in a much more placid current the heavily laden and populated craft gently floated onward and downstream toward Canada. That it did so in stately if not speedy fashion is attested to by John's account that it took them seven days to cover the 35 miles to Okinook (now Porthill), immediately south of the border.

They had almost reached their goal—the flats of the Kootenay River in Canada were in sight before them—but first they had to prepare themselves for the winter that was closing in upon them. Although they likely either sold or left some of the cattle in Kalispell with John Arrowsmith, they did take most of the animals on to Bonners Ferry, and herding them would have been a problem without two of the oldest males, but these frontier women were adaptable. James probably did the herding with the girls, while the mother drove the light wagon.

The value of the reconnaissance trip that William and James had made a month or two earlier, while the rest stayed on in Kalispell, was now evident in the form of a relic of the past which they had found on that foray: an old Hudson's Bay Company fort. It was inevitable that the Huscrofts would eventually make contact with the HBC, even if it was only in the form of an ancient stronghold inhabited by ghosts.

In 1808, David Thompson, North West Company surveyor, explorer and trader, had travelled between the sites of what were to be Libby, Montana, and Bonners Ferry, Idaho, using what he called in his journal a well-trodden trail. (If nothing else, this proved that the first inhabitants of that countryside were wise enough not to attempt that stretch of the river with their canoes.) When he reached Bonners Ferry, Thompson launched his river craft and went downstream to Kootenay Lake, which he reported on and looked at, but did not explore, then returned to Bonners Ferry and went upstream from there to the Kootenay's confluence with the Moyie River. He followed that valley north to the site of present-day Cranbrook, B.C., then crossed over to the Columbia and back to the prairie. Sometime later (it's not clear whether it was before or after the HBC bought out the North Westers), a post was built near Okinook and named Fort Flatbow (this was probably inspired by Thompson's journal). Long before the 1890s it was discontinued and deserted, and after the company lost its land tenure in B.C., it was open to all.[13]

The Huscrofts' father and son either found the fort or heard of it in Bonners Ferry, and it was there that the Huscroft family stayed for their first winter beside the Kootenay River. Whether Fort Flatbow was in B.C. or Idaho is an unanswered question, as James Huscroft says it was his recollection that they crossed the border on September 1, 1891, before that first winter.

In any case, as soon as the sloughs froze they could ride cross-country to Bonners Ferry for supplies, which they did on two occasions, and they sent out news of their progress to mother Emma Fisher and to son George in Provo, and to John Arrowsmith in Kalispell. On these trips they likely brought their herd of horses and cattle from Bonners Ferry, where they would have had to leave them before rafting to Porthill. The Arrowsmiths joined them early in 1892, and that year saw them all finally settled in Canada, less George and family, who joined them in 1894.

Southern B.C. had just entered the most exciting period of its history, and if William Rodger Huscroft anticipated finding unspoiled wilderness, he was out of luck, his timing off by at least 10 years.[14] The opening of the Canadian Pacific Railway main line in 1886 started up a general interest in the far western province, but it was the discovery of lead, zinc and silver in substantial quantities in many places along and close to the international boundary, from the Okanagan Valley to the Rocky Mountains, that really put things into high gear, with the resulting human ingress coming almost exclusively from the United States.

Small numbers of these American immigrants might have been pioneers interested in tilling the land, like the Huscrofts, but the overwhelming majority of them were prospectors and miners, and of course they were accompanied by the promoters and manipulators associated with that industry. There were also pioneer railway builders plying their trade, and at the start they also came from the United States.

This mining frenzy started in 1883 when an old pick-and-pan prospector found colour in the Coeur d'Alene Range about 100 miles south of the line in Idaho Territory. This gold rush was followed by larger finds of other minerals, and those discovering them soon turned their footsteps north.

In 1887 the Hall brothers claimed outcrops of copper and silver on Toad Mountain, some nine miles from Nelson, resulting in the Silver King Mine, and this was followed by similar discoveries at Ainsworth alongside Kootenay Lake in 1889, at Rossland near Trail in 1890, and in the Slocan area in 1891. The Payne Mine in the latter district quickly became the greatest dividend payer in the province.

The Huscroft family arrived right at the start of this mining extravaganza, when the curtain was still rising, and the scene was now set for William, Jane and their children to present themselves at the customs house just inside the Canadian border, where the Kootenay River flows in northbound. The locale was named after the customs officer there, one J.C. Rykerts, an ex-North West Mounted Policeman who had come to B.C. in 1882, as one of the guard for the Marquis of Lorne, the Canadian

Kootenay Lake and Creston Flats

Governor General, and stayed. He was one of a cohort of purveyors of all
government services at entry points to B.C. from the south, which also
included such worthies as J.C. Hayne, who later became a judge, and Peter
O'Reilly, who subsequently became gold commissioner.[15]

Like his illustrious colleagues, whom he never equalled in glory
attained nor land acquired through the position, Rykerts was customs
officer, immigration inspector and gold commissioner's agent. In this
place he was also the registrar of shipping. He was obviously a man who
could greatly help the Huscrofts, and he did. He also became a friend,
giving them the logs for their first cabin.

A New Land of Promise

Once suitably admitted to the country, the family proceeded to build
a log cabin across the river, presumably within the purview, and the
dyking, of what was called The English Reclamation Company. The
Huscroft men were grateful to obtain employment with that company,
and they carried out all the essentials of pioneer living: building a cabin,
cultivating vegetables, growing hay for the animals and so on. They no
longer had to depend on their own efforts to obtain mail and supplies
from Bonners Ferry because Charlie Davis and the *Midge* were not only

servicing the reclamation operation, they were also running a supply service to the miners at the recently opened Bluebell Mine at Riondel, located halfway up Kootenay Lake, as well as to the Huscrofts, and the supplies for that came from Bonners Ferry.

John Arrowsmith and his family joined them in 1896, taking up land adjoining the flats farther upstream, close to the site of the future township of Creston.[16] Arrowsmith is said to have arrived with only one horse, the other three of the four pulling his wagon having died on the trip.

George Huscroft, who had stayed behind in Provo, came north in 1893, starting his family in Bonners Ferry. They settled in Kaslo, where the next year he and his wife, Mary, added another to their brood. Later they also moved to the Creston area.

All proceeded quite nicely throughout 1892 and 1893, and in these years another and much more elegant vessel was plying the river past them. This was the SS *Nelson*, a sternwheeler of fine lines and rather exceptional horsepower, which from time to time was towing barges loaded with galena, the heaviest ore (a mixture of lead, zinc and silver), which was then being shovelled out of the ground at the Payne Mine and other mining properties near Sandon in the Slocan district. (The miners also, initially, found it lying in boulders on the surface at some sites.) The *Nelson* was towing the barges upstream to Bonners Ferry, where its load would be transferred to the Great Northern Railway, whose right-of-way the Huscrofts had traversed in 1891. That railway was now in operation under its president, J.J. Hill, a dedicated opponent to the CPR's W.C. Van Horne.[17]

Things did not go quite so smoothly for the Huscrofts in 1894. With more snow than normal, the winter of 1893–94 was a very severe one, but that was something these hardy settlers could take. What disturbed our pioneering family much more profoundly was what happened when the snow melted.

One morning in the spring of 1894, as they sat down to breakfast in their rough-built log cabin beside the river, water appeared on the floor. It flowed in rapidly and unceasingly. Their neighbours came to the rescue. One of these was Charlie Davis, with his sturdy steam launch the *Midge*. He arrived at their waterlogged doorstep towing a reclamation company barge.[18] Gratefully they loaded everything transportable in the cabin, including the still-dismantled wagons, onto the barge, and they were towed to high-water mark ... and then to high-water mark again ... and again, until the Kootenay finally stopped rising. It was the worst snow-melt flood in B.C.'s history. It is said that at Creston that spring the river rose to a point eight feet above any height that it had ever reached before—far above Baillie-Grohman's dykes, which suffered seriously. It is also said that the Huscrofts had the greatest difficulty getting the stove through the cabin door, as they had built the cabin around the stove.

The Huscrofts had to build again, and they immediately started looking for a new place to settle. The topography of the Kootenay River valley from Creston south to the U.S. border, as you move from west to east, consists of the continuous steep slopes of the Selkirk Mountains on the west side, then the river flats, then a bench of relatively flat land three to four miles wide and 50 to 100 feet above the river. This stretches to the east boundary of the valley, where lies a most scenic escarpment of the Purcell Mountains.[19] (Both the Purcells and the Selkirks are ranges of the Columbia Mountains.) The bench was heavily wooded in parts, but almost all of it could be satisfactorily cultivated (when the trees were removed) to grow orchards in the north and alfalfa in the south, as time would tell. The family built a road up to this bench, at the south end, and settled there. They and the road are still there. The area of the bench eventually became known as Lister. Some of it was also known as Huscroft.

It was fitting that a carry-over from Baillie-Grohman's vision, in the form of a steam launch, should help William Huscroft realize his dreams, as it was likely Baillie-Grohman's writing that triggered Huscroft's move from Utah. But neither the *Midge* nor its new owner fared well in the 1894 flood—both of them disappeared.

John Huscroft, William's son, eventually spotted the *Midge* lying on the bottom of the Kootenay River near the Bonners Ferry dock, fully covered in silt (Davis did not sink with it; he left the valley). The silt preserved it, and the faithful craft was pulled out some years later, refloated, and rather unkindly renamed the *Mudhen*. It did not last long as that, however, and soon it met a permanent watery grave on the bottom of the same river close to the West Creston ferry.

Now that they were established on dry land, it only remained for the Huscroft men to put their hands to it, and they certainly did. In

This 1909 photo shows the house the Huscrofts built on the Huscroft Bench. On the extreme right is William Rodger Huscroft. Huscroft, an orphan from Yorkshire, England, was a member of a diminishing agricultural community that in the mid-1800s was forced by the Industrial Revolution into a life in town or city made unbearable by filth and disease. His future wife, Jane Fisher (inset, with grandson Bill), came from Bedfordshire, England. Like Huscroft, her parents joined the Mormon Church and moved to the United States. She and William met there and married some years later.

On Huscroft's right is his son Charles. In the doorway is his son John, followed by John's wife Monna Wigen (who died in 1913) and William's daughter Maud. The child is daughter Sarah's boy, Ernest Ennerson Jr. (Sarah died in childbirth in 1904.)

John had two children with his first wife. After Monna died, he married Amy Johnson and fathered seven more. Charles married Penelope (Nelly) Waddy, a schoolteacher who came from Calgary in 1913, and they had seven children. Maud married Tom Ross and they had eight. It rounded out at two dozen for all three.

Both Jane and William eventually rejected the Mormon Church. They moved to British Columbia in 1891.

two generations they became land-clearing and stump-blasting experts, loggers, sawyers, hay farmers, wheat growers, orchardists, cattle ranchers and dairy farmers. They built houses, barns, sheds and workshops, fences, roads, water systems and drainage ditches (even irrigation ditches, which John learned about in Utah). They also worked for the Great Northern Railway, building the line to Kuskanook, and on early public roads in the area.

From horsemen and teamsters they became truck drivers and tractor and bulldozer and combine operators. To maintain their equipment they became blacksmiths, welders, mechanics, woodworkers, plumbers and electricians. They raised horses, cattle, sheep, pigs, chickens, geese and turkeys. To care for and deal with their animals and land they became part-time and non-professional veterinarians, pest and vermin exterminators, butchers, agriculturists, weather forecasters and much more.

And what of the women? Well of course they had this business of procreating, and initially no means of controlling it, and no doctors, drugstores or district nurses. These would come very slowly. In the beginning they had no running water or indoor toilets (and sometimes a long way to carry water). They had primitive lighting and heating, very little in the way of laundry facilities and cooking utensils, but many mouths to feed and clothes to wash, and babies and young ones to care for and cherish. They bound up their children's, and their menfolk's, wounds and treated their aches, colds, measles and whooping cough.

Blessedly there was no cholera or such, but there was blood poisoning and pneumonia, bone fractures and head injuries, which were constant threats to men working with sharp tools and primitive machines in rough and hard conditions and weather. The women knew all about these—the injured fell into their laps. And besides all of this, these women sewed, knitted, canned and bottled fruit and vegetables, baked, cooked, celebrated Christmas, Easter and Thanksgiving, taught their offspring the golden rule, and gave their spouses love and encouragement! They earned their keep.

Thus a pioneer family in British Columbia was established—and a large one. All the eight offspring who stayed in or around Lister had families of an average size of six and a half—in other words, they produced 52 grandchildren, who in turn produced 120 great-grandchildren. On

The Unlocking

William Adolf Baillie-Grohman left the Kootenays forever in 1891, but tangible results of his B.C. sojourn lasted for at least 10 years after. In 1889, as part of the agreement he had with the province, he turned over to it the canal he had constructed at Canal Flats. It was 6,700 feet long, 45 feet wide, built to contain a minimum depth of 4 feet, and was equipped with one lock, 100 feet long by 30 feet wide. The canal connected the Kootenay River to Columbia Lake. The Kootenay was on average about five feet above the lake at that point. Within three years the whole reclamation scheme collapsed as both the provincial and federal governments rejected it, and in the great flood of 1894 the canal and the lock were seriously damaged and virtually abandoned.

This did not deter the riverboat industry in the Kootenays. In 1901, Captain F.P. Armstrong was inspired by the discovery of ore on Toby Creek in the upper Columbia region to start planning the transfer of the sternwheeler SS *North Star* from the upper Kootenay to the upper Columbia. The problem was that the *North Star* was 130 feet long, the lock basin was 30 feet shorter, and the opening of the lock gates was nine inches too narrow. Not to worry: they took the rubbing strip off the vessel to solve the width problem. As for the lock-basin length, their answer was both ingenious and daring.

At a suitable distance downstream from the lower gate, they built a dam of ore bags filled with sand. They removed the lower lock gates, which were made of timber, by burning them. They then impounded enough water behind their new barrier to float the *North Star* into the lock, built another sandbagged barrier beside the upper gate to protect against inrush by the Kootenay, and after raising the water level sufficiently in their new lock, they blasted out the lower barrier. In the resultant rush of sand and water, the *North Star* was disgorged into Columbia Lake with minimum damage. The canal was then completely filled in. The crew of the new arrival on the Columbia River navigated it north to Golden, where they were treated to a sumptuous banquet by the local populace.[20]

August 2, 1991, almost exactly 100 years from the day the family ended the raft trip down the river from Bonners Ferry, the Huscrofts held a reunion. There were around 300 descendants in attendance.

For this they built a small-scale replica of the raft, made of slightly smaller logs and bereft of cargo, but with handrails and an outboard motor attached. They launched it in a side slough to the Kootenay River, which had not quite got over its summer high water, and all that day, to the amazement of American tourists on the nearby highway, a succession of Huscrofts paid their respects to William Rodger and to John Henry, his son, by emulation. The reunion went on until August 4.[21]

William and Jane lived out their lives quietly after their sons and daughters married and moved away from them. Sarah Etta, their fifth daughter, died giving birth to her first child in 1904, when living in Rexford, Montana. Her husband, Ernest Ennerson, stayed on in the United States, and he remarried in 1926. In the interim his son was raised by Jane Huscroft. After all, she had already raised 11, so that was nothing new, although by then she was 63 years of age. One son moved to Florida due to asthma and repeated pneumonia bouts from the colder weather in Canada, but most stayed nearby. Jane died in 1918 when she was 77, and William in 1922, aged 92. Son John said that if only the old man had found a substantial interest or a cause to fight for, he would have lived to be 100.

Yorkshire, Bedfordshire and Utah were the lesser to lose William and Jane Huscroft, and Canada and B.C. the greater to gain them.

Memories of Charles Leroy Huscroft

Charles took time to assess new acquaintances and accept them. In my case it was done even less speedily than usual due to my Scottish upbringing and my early life as a city dweller in Glasgow. He did put up with my complete ignorance of Canadian farming life and customs once he had decided that I was genuine in my desire to conform and that I was not a two-timer, a loudmouth or a city slicker—his major dislikes.

In time I was pleased to accept some rye whisky and water, slowly and jointly consumed, mostly in silence. If questioned about the old times in the right way—I am most interested in history—he would speak of the very early years, but usually reluctantly. He gave details of the family's entrance into British Columbia, the difficulties of removing stumps and the problems with flooding (which caused the move to Lister Bench), and he sometimes spoke of difficulties with the Natives.

He recalled the way the U.S. Army handled the Kootenai Nation when members became obstreperous. The soldiers watched them and noted who were the most talkative. Then they befriended one of those outgoing types (who was a chief) and took him on a trip to the eastern seaboard, where they showed him the army's latest weapons—in those days it was the Gatling gun—and made sure he understood that if his band members continued to give trouble, then these weapons, and more soldiers, would quickly be brought to the Kootenays, with dire result. They then returned the chief to his people. It worked. He never stopped talking about all that he had seen, and the soldiers had little trouble after that. It was a triumph for psychology, and likely the sort of thing that Charles himself would have thought of had he been in that situation.

He was a man of great personal dignity, with a keen mind, a deep interest in life and people (at least those who met his standards), and under it all an underplayed but intriguing sense of humour. Someone difficult to get to know, but most rewarding to converse with when you did.

(Charles died in 1968.)

This was written by R.G. Harvey in 1951, after becoming Charles Leroy Huscroft's son-in-law.

Our Pioneers

In history if we could turn back a page
We would find our forebears in a rugged age,
With things so different than we have today
No modern things to ease the way.

Their shoes were neither left nor right
They'd swap them 'round at bed each night.
Their clothes were cumbersome away back when
No wash-and-wear nor spandex then.

From lye and ashes they made their soap
And water was hauled from a well with a rope
Or carried in buckets from nearby stream
Our gleaming showers were a future dream.

And electric lights? No never for them
It was tallow candles way back then.
No jets to speed them on their way.
No trains or cars to ease their way.

No super highways ribboned the land.
No 911 nor phone at hand.
Their only help for each day's demands
Was the end of their arms—their own two hands.

If our forebears ever look down on us
They must wonder why we make a fuss
And complain at all of our daily lot
When compared to them we have such a lot.

Compared to them we live like kings
Beyond their dreams, if their dreams had wings.
But they loved and laughed and did their best,
They opened the land so our lives were blessed.

To express my thanks, I can only begin —
We owe so much to our pioneer kin.

Shirley M. Edis (née Huscroft)

TURNING AN ENGINEER INTO AN AUTHOR

Before going into the details of how an engineer became an author, I should say something about those who really knew what they were doing in recording the history of British Columbia.

Two groups have dominated. The first of these is the academic fraternity, the university professors. The acknowledged bible of historical writing in B.C. is *British Columbia: A History* by Margaret A. Ormsby, who was a professor of history at the University of British Columbia. This great book was commissioned by the provincial government to mark the centenary of British Columbia in 1958. Margaret Ormsby died a few years ago, but her book has remained unsurpassed as the leading history of this province.

Still with university professors, there is a husband-and-wife team, both of that calling, Gordon and Helen Akrigg.[1] They produced two remarkable volumes relating pre-colonial and colonial history, *The British Columbia Chronicles*, covering the years 1778 to 1871. They also produced a handy helper to those studying B.C., a book called *1001 British Columbia Place Names*, which has had repeated editions. This not only lists a huge number of place names, but also gives a few paragraphs, or half a page, of the history of each. This is a priceless help to anyone writing about our province.

The second group is made up of what could be called "the institutional historians." These are writers who are employed by such institutions as the British Columbia Museum, the Provincial Archives, or our provincial newspapers. Leading among them is Robert D. Turner, who was chief of historical collections at the B.C. Provincial Museum and is now retired as curator emeritus. He has produced a magnificent history of sternwheelers and steam tugs, mostly those of the CPR. He has also written of the *Princesses*, the CPR coastal vessels, and of the *Empresses*, the passenger liners that sailed around the world under that company's flag.

Turner's predecessor in the field of river and lake transportation in this province was Norman R. Hacking, who was for many years the marine editor of the Vancouver *Province*. He wrote a wonderful series of articles for the *British Columbia Historical Quarterly*, a provincial government publication that is now moribund. Hacking entertains us with his colourful accounts of the sternwheelers and of the men who piloted them on the lakes and rivers of B.C.

These academic and institutional authors had one great help in their efforts—they were professionals in what they wrote about. Ormsby and the Akriggs were generalists, each in their own format. Turner and Hacking were specialists in the marine field. All of them helped develop a theme discussed here, which is consistent in all the books I have written so far—the history of the various transportation corridors through the mountains and plateaus of the B.C. Interior.

I have met only one other civil engineer in the course of this writing. He was a bridge engineer from Vancouver by the name of R.C. Harris. Richard Harris, who died a few years ago, was what could be called a "small turf" historian—he specialized in the fur brigade trails across the Cascade Mountains in B.C. and little else. He viewed any words written on these trails with a piercing gaze, and he quickly pointed out any inaccuracies. In correspondence he finally came through as a friend deserving of great admiration.

Harris wrote an excellent article about the first Alexandra Bridge over the Fraser River in the canyon, which appeared in the *B.C. Historical News* in 1982. It is the best available source of information on that historic structure, and it is very well researched and presented. He also forwarded a reproduction of a report made by Sapper James Turnbull of the Royal Engineers, which describes his exploration of the Coquihalla valley in 1862.[2]

Now to relate my own conjuncture with this learned company. One day in the late 1970s, Bill Bennett, the premier, phoned the deputy minister of highways (me) to advise that his brother and his sister were both members of the Kelowna Chamber of Commerce, which was having its annual meeting in the next week or two. They wanted someone to talk about the Okanagan Highway. He asked if I could do it, and, as you don't turn down premiers, I agreed that I would.

I immediately asked the highways department chief clerk, a man called Frank Howland, to bring me everything that he could find out about the Okanagan Highway. Frank had started in Highways when he was 16 years old, and he was then on the brink of retirement—there was very little that he did not know about highways in British Columbia. He soon walked in with a stack of file folders about four feet high.

Amazingly this included some records dating back to 1908, the year the Department of Public Works came into existence. I asked if he had any other files, such as for the Fraser Canyon Road, and he produced the file for that road which included correspondence with the CPR going back to the 1880s and earlier. This was not just background on a highway; this was historic documentation from the early years of the province.

When I congratulated him on this trove, he said, "Well, you had better enjoy it now, because this material will not be with us for long." Questioned on this, he told of a program to microfilm old files and then destroy the originals. He showed a sample of the reproduced images from the Hope-Princeton Highway file, which had already been done, and they were dreadful. This microfilming was being carried out by another ministry, and the people deciding what should be kept and what should be discarded were often ignorant of the documents' great historic value.

We decided that this was not good enough, and Frank said, "You tell me which of these old files you want kept, and I will simply hide them." He said we should only keep those from before the Second World War. I agreed to this and gave him a list of the essential files. I also cautioned him to pass on the details of his hiding place to his successor.

Well, I gave the talk and it seemed to be well received. Some years later, another highways minister, Alec Fraser, gave me a series of assignments to cushion the shock of the idleness of retirement.[3] One of these was to monitor the construction of the Coquihalla Highway and to write a report on it when it was finished. This is an excellent highway, quite remarkable both for the challenge of its terrain and for the short time allowed for its construction—75 miles were built through the Cascade Mountains in two years at the whim of a premier. Since it opened in 1986 it has been an outstanding money-maker for B.C. politicians as a toll facility. In fact it probably won't be too many years before it recoups the millions they wasted on the fast ferries—a recent fiasco in British Columbia's transportation history.

At any rate, I wrote the report and fleshed it out with some history from the files, which were retrieved from Frank's hiding place and eventually returned with the recommendation that they be handed over to the Provincial Archives. Alec Fraser returned the report, and he gave his permission for its unrestricted use.

It was not long enough for publication on its own, so the idea came to combine it with the history of similar outlets to the coast from the Interior of B.C.—the Hope-Princeton Highway, the Fraser Canyon Highway and so on. This is how my first book, *The Coast Connection*, was born. The initial conception was to rebut Premier Vander Zalm's criticism of Bennett's highway, but as the writing progressed it became more and more historical.

When something is done once, it is much easier to do it again, and in due course another book came out, which the publisher turned into two—*Carving*

the Western Path By River, Rail, and Road Through B.C.'s Southern Mountains and
*Carving the Western Path By River, Rail, and Road Through Central and Northern
B.C.* Here the focus was widened to include railways as well as highways, and it
also included those remarkable old riverboats, the sternwheelers, a wonderful
part of B.C.'s transportation history. It covered the whole province.

In all of this writing I made extensive use of the precious old files
providentially saved by Frank Howland. There was another treasure chest of
facts and figures from the past thanks to another old-timer, H.T. Miard, deputy
minister of highways from 1958 to 1973. He hired two university students for
summer work one year, and he had the brilliant idea of sending them to the
Provincial Archives in Victoria and telling them to dig out all the information
they could find about the history of the highways department. He told them to
make copies of all the documents they could uncover, especially the very early
ones. The result was a loose-leaf folder about two inches thick, full of photostat
copies. Frank threw this in along with the files.

Most of this early material from colonial and early provincial days was
handwritten correspondence, finely scribed, rather poorly reproduced and
very difficult to read. I went through every page, and that took a great deal of
time. I found that a computer was helpful for this task, as I could decipher the
files, type them into the computer and then print them out for easier reference.
This material proved to be a godsend for further writing as it provided the
essential ingredients you must have if you want to get into this business of
writing history—facts and information, and preferably the correct facts and
the right information. These are an indispensable part of writing non-fiction,
and if you don't have the material, forget it.

The old files and records had to be read and reread, suggesting that a
course in how to read quickly could be a great help. I was fortunate to be living
in Victoria, with access to the main public library there. It is a wonderful source
of information on the history of this province. I was fortunate, too, to have as a
neighbour an old Mountie who had served all over British Columbia in his long
career, extending over 40 years, and who, everywhere he went, had collected
books about that area of the province, many of them now long out of print.
When he died, his wife very kindly donated these to me. This kind of generosity
is a marvellous help to any writer of B.C. history.

The bibliographies of each of my four books list 75 volumes or more.
Allowing for overlap, the research involved reading about 150 books in a
period of six years. Some of them I only perused in part, but most of them
were read right through. Not only reading is necessary. The historian must also
carefully note and reference everything that is taken from the books, and here
something should be said about this business of referencing.

When writing about history, you cannot simply make a statement and let it rest at that. If you do, other historians will say that you have fabricated it. You have to indicate where you learned that fact. Here is an example. In one book I report that Colonel R.C. Moody of the Royal Engineers walked out into the Cascades one day and looked at Allison Pass, which had just been discovered by John Allison. He then wrote to Governor Douglas and observed that it would be a good way through the mountains for a railway.

It was then necessary to append a tiny superscripted number, which referred to the same numbered entry in the chapter notes for that chapter, and these notes contained this: "Letter dated August 23, 1860, from Lieutenant Colonel Richard Moody, R.E., to His Honour, Governor James Douglas. Department of Lands and Works File 151, letter written at Hope, B.C." This was one of the letters that had been tediously transcribed.

I visited the Provincial Archives many times to research documents on such subjects as the Alaska Highway in British Columbia. I searched their visual records files for photographs, using their computers and via their Internet connection. I discovered many photographs that way, including several wrongly filed, and I paid a reproduction fee and paid for permission to publish them. These photographs also had to be fully referenced.

After the first book was written, and published, the reaction set in. There were letters. Fortunately I can choose which I want to mention. Some came from those rather tiresome correspondents, nitpickers—there are lots of them, and every author hears from them. One even took the book to task because it failed to modernize the name of a town. Spences Bridge was spelled with an apostrophe, as it would have been written before 1900. In 1900 the Cartographers Association of Canada outlawed the possessive form for place names in our country, and the context of this reference was a few years after that. So the apostrophe was out of order.

But the letters received were not all bad—there were some nice ones, especially one from a lovely woman in Penticton, Mrs. Kathryn Buchanan. She wrote and said that she enjoyed the book, particularly the mention of the Royal Engineers, that adventurous band of civil engineers and sappers who built the first Fraser Canyon Road before there even was a province of British Columbia. Mrs. Buchanan wrote that when she was a little girl, in 1923, her parents took her to Penticton for a holiday, and when she walked back and forth to town, she got to know a very old lady tending her garden. They conversed, and the lady told her that she was the widow of Lieutenant Henry Spencer Palmer of the Royal Engineers.

Palmer was the point man for Colonel Moody. It was Palmer who explored the new colony with the Hudson's Bay men. He sought alternative routes to the coast from the Interior, and he wrote a very fine report of his trip from Fort Alexandria to Bella Coola, following in the footsteps of Alexander Mackenzie. As did other officers of the detachment, he found a wife in the colony, and he took her with him when he left in 1863.

Palmer later died in the Philippines, and his wife, a clergyman's daughter, returned to British Columbia. That fine lady, 60 years later, confided to my correspondent that when they were married, Colonel Moody gave them a choice of wedding presents. One was an oil painting and the other a tract of land. As they were leaving the colony, they chose the painting. The land is now a large part of Stanley Park.

When I read a letter like this, it conveys a sense of stretching 140 years back into the past, to the very start of this province and into the time of its wonderful pioneers. The hand that wrote that letter touched the hand of Lieutenant Palmer's wife.

It has always been the people, the individuals, who are of most interest to me in the history of this province, and there has been no lack of interesting characters. Mackenzie and Mann were an intriguing pair, for example. Entrepreneurs and operators—some said "close to the wind"—they took part in Canada's follow-up railways, the ones after the CPR, although often only on paper.

Then there were the great sternwheeler captains and owners—William Moore and John Irving. Who could ask for men more enterprising than they? The list grows—Walter Moberley and Joseph Trutch, Colonel Moody and Governor Douglas, William Van Horne and Major Rogers, Jim Hill and Andrew McCulloch, Andrew Onderdonk and Michael Haney. If you do not know of them, read of them. These were men to admire. There were also men to admire among the road crews, as described in several of my books.

In closing I must say I have little patience for people who claim to have no interest in the past, and who say they are only interested in the present. These are people who do not know that they are a leaf from a tree—and you can learn a great deal from that tree!

Michael Crichton, author of *Jurassic Park* and many other popular novels, has said: "The past has always been more important than the present. The present is like a coral island that sticks out above the water, but is built upon millions of dead corals under the surface that no one sees. In the same way our everyday world is built upon millions and millions of events and decisions that occurred in the past. And what we add in the present is trivial."

In any case, people should buy more books about history.

This ends the story of an engineer being turned into an author.

Road Men of the North

It is almost impossible to work for the road authority in British Columbia without meeting some interesting characters, and the farther north you go, the more interesting they are. I fondly remember a much-liked foreman by the name of Ted Arnoldus, who was in charge of the Honeymoon Creek camp on the Hart Highway. He had trouble with the English language, as Casey Stengel did. He was worried about some farmers ditching to bring water to their land, and he phoned me in order to, in his words, "discuss them irritation ditches!"

Patrick O'Toole was the superintendent at Fort St. John in the early 1960s. He was probably the only government official ever to be honoured by a large group of citizens petitioning the government in Victoria to grant a special day of leave to a provincial civil servant on his birthday. Pat was born on St. Patrick's Day. The locals liked him. Every year they put on a birthday celebration to honour him; every year he was called away on a road emergency — they wanted a law against it.

Jock Rattray was the foreman in charge of the Good Hope Lake camp on the Cassiar-Stewart highway near Watson Lake, and he was into everything. When a toddler broke an arm and the father was out of camp, child and mother were immediately driven to the hospital at Cassiar with Jock at the wheel. That it was far below zero with driving snow and a partial whiteout when the accident happened mattered little.

Good Hope Lake, a happy camp, depended on the Tahltan Native Band, and a finer group of people could not be found. Most of the non-Native men had Native wives, and when the local school district hired an out-of-province immigrant as the schoolteacher at Good Hope Lake, his wife very soon split the camp on racial lines. When this, and the usual bush fever in the spring, led to the inevitable explosion, Jock Rattray told the couple to be in their mobile house trailer one morning, ready to leave. He hooked the trailer to a department truck and towed it, and them, right down to Edmonton, where they were originally hired, and he left them there. He was a man of simple solutions.

These men need to be remembered.

List of Events of Historical Relevance

1792 Captain Robert Gray finds the mouth of the Columbia River. An American, he names it after his ship.

1807–09 David Thompson travels through the Rocky Mountains by Howse Pass and the Blaeberry River to the Columbia River. Assuming it flows north, he ascends it southward to its source and founds Kootenae House at the outlet of Windermere Lake. He then follows the Kootenay River to where it turns west and then north, where he founds Kootenae Fort. He leaves it and moves south founding Flathead Fort, Saleesh House, Kullyspell House (Kalispel) and Spokane House. He then goes west to the Columbia at Kettle Falls and ascends it to the Blaeberry and back through the Rockies.

1810–11 Thompson is unable to use Howse Pass due to opposing Peigans. He finds another pass through the Rockies, Athabasca Pass, which brings him to the Columbia at Boat Encampment. He retraces his earlier route to Kootenae House, Spokane House, Kettle Falls and downstream from there. He has to portage at Celilo Falls and Cascade Falls, both downstream of the Snake River. He founds Fort Nez Perce at the confluence of the Snake. He meets the Americans at Astoria and returns upstream to Boat Encampment, thus becoming the first European to ascend the full length of the Columbia.

1811 Men from John Jacob Astor's Pacific Fur Company reach the mouth of the Columbia River by sea.

1812 The Americans sell Astoria to the Hudson's Bay Company for $58,000.

1820 The HBC starts using the route from Kamloops to Fort Okanogan and down the Columbia to tidewater.

1821 The HBC buys out the North West Company.

1825 The HBC founds Fort Vancouver near the mouth of the Columbia, abandons Spokane House and builds Fort Colville near the confluence of the Okanagan River. The HBC establishes Fort Langley near the mouth of the Fraser River.

1827 The United States and Canada agree to a joint occupation of Oregon.

1843 James Douglas of the HBC establishes Fort Victoria on Vancouver Island.

1846 The international boundary is set along the 49th parallel by treaty.

1847 The last HBC fur brigade comes down the Columbia to tidewater.

1850–58 Steamboat service is established on the upper Columbia.

1856 HBC closes Fort Colville (which becomes Marcus, Washington) and starts up Fort Sheppard, north of the 49th parallel on the Columbia.

1864 Gold is found at Wild Horse Creek, and Bonners Ferry, Idaho, is established. The Walla Walla Trail is extended into Canada.

1865 The Big Bend of the Columbia gold rush. Walter Moberly finds Eagle Pass, an easy access to the Columbia River from Shuswap Lake. The SS *Forty Nine* is launched at Marcus, lined through the Little Dalles and enters Lower Arrow Lake to start steamboat service on the south flow of the Columbia River.

1866 Moberly builds a trail from Seymour Arm of Shuswap Lake to Big Eddy, future site of Revelstoke, and Captain Houghton goes ahead with a trail from Vernon to Edgewood to replace "Moberly's vile trail." The first steamboat, the SS *Marten*, is launched on Shuswap Lake.

1871 The Province of British Columbia is founded as part of Canada.

1875 A road is built from Nicola Lake to Kamloops.

1883 Gustavus Blin Wright builds a road from Shuswap Lake and Mara Lake to Revelstoke. Wright also provides a ferry across the Columbia at Revelstoke.

1886 The CPR transcontinental line is finished. A road is built from Spence's Bridge easterly to Nicola, Princeton, Osoyoos and Penticton.

1886–87 A road is built from Galbraith's Ferry to Canal Flats, and a bridge is built there. Settlement spreads from Shuswap Lake southwards.

1887 Ore is found at Nelson. The Northern Pacific Railway opens its transcontinental line to Oregon in the United States. The nearest point to B.C. is Sandpoint, Idaho.

1887–91 Roads are built from Monte Creek to Salmon Arm, and from Osoyoos easterly.

1890 The first train of the Spokane Falls and Northern Railway reaches Marcus and Little Dalles from Spokane, Washington. Two years later the line is extended to Fort Sheppard.

1891 Ore is found at Red Mountain near Rossland.

1892 The rail line from Sicamous to Okanagan Landing, the Shuswap and Okanagan Railway, is fully operational, and is soon purchased by the CPR.

1893 The Great Northern Railway transcontinental line to Tacoma, Washington, is opened. The line goes through Bonners Ferry, Idaho. The Nelson and Fort Sheppard Railway is opened.

1895–97 The Eagle Pass road is rebuilt after being destroyed by the CPR, and the Enderby to Revelstoke road is rebuilt. A road is built from Moyie to Cranbrook and Fort Steele.

1897–98 The CPR builds the Crows Nest Railway, and Creston becomes a rail point.

1898 A road is built from Cranbrook to Jaffray and Elko. The CPR purchases the Columbia and Western Railway and the Trail smelter from Auguste Heinze. The SS *Moyie* is launched at Nelson.

1900 The first Good Roads Association branch in B.C. is formed. The GN Railway takes over the SF&N Railway. The CPR lays track from Proctor, along the West Arm of Kootenay Lake, to Nelson.

1907 A through road is completed from Creston to Fernie.

1908 Travellers promoting roads go by trail from Kamloops to Little Fort, Valemont and Tete Jaune Cache and by the Canoe River to Boat Encampment and on to Donald and then by "comfortable wagon road" to Fort Steele. The town of Fernie is destroyed by fire. The Department of Public Works of B.C. is separated from the Lands Department and is headed by a minister in place of a commissioner.

1911 The first Alexandra Bridge is demolished, and Premier McBride and public works minister Thomas Taylor start on a southern trans-provincial route from Hope by Gibson Pass to Penticton, Osoyoos, Nelson and Fernie. The Hope to Princeton by Gibson Pass road is abandoned in 1918.

1912 A bridge is built over the Columbia River at Trail.

1913 The province abandons the Banff–Windermere road, and the Dominion government takes it over. The SS *Nasookin* is launched at Nelson.

1914 The gap in the Okanagan Highway between Westbank and Peachland is filled in. The SS *Sicamous* is launched on Okanagan Lake.

1916 The Coquihalla Pass rail line is completed in July. Three months before that, J.J. Hill dies. Both the KVR and the GN commence operations on the Coquihalla Pass line.

1923 The CPR opens a line from Penticton to Osoyoos with rail transfer barge service on Skaha Lake.

1924–26 The second Alexandra Bridge is built.

1925 The Canadian National Railway opens a line from Kamloops to Kelowna and starts tug and barge service on Okanagan Lake.

1927 B.C. signs a shared-cost agreement for the construction of the Big Bend Highway and the Kootenay Columbia Highway with Ottawa. The Department of Public Works is reported to have 18 gas shovels, 50 power graders, 100 tractors and 250 trucks. At this time, pneumatic tires and antifreeze mixes are introduced for motor vehicles.

1928 The road from Yale to Spences Bridge is completed. (The Yale to Lytton section opened the year before.) A road is opened from Golden eastwards to Yoho National Park, and the Dominion government opens a road from Yoho to Alberta.

1929–30 B.C. signs an agreement for joint construction of the Big Bend Highway with the Dominion government, with 50 percent of the roadwork paid for by Ottawa. A road is built from Cranbrook to Kimberley and on to Golden, with an offshoot to Vermilion Pass.

1930 The SS *Kuskanook's* tri-weekly service from Nelson to Kaslo is stopped. The rail line from Kootenay Landing to Proctor is opened, and the SS *Nasookin* is leased to the Department of Public Works as a highway ferry.

1931 Steam tugs *Valhalla* and *Hosmer* are sold by the CPR at Nelson. A rail line is opened to replace the rail transfer barge service on Skaha Lake, and this starts the CPR's departure from lake transport on Okanagan Lake. The CPR officially takes over the Kettle Valley Railway. Forest fires ravage the B.C. Interior.

1932 Relief camp work starts on the Big Bend Highway and the Hope–Princeton Highway. By year's end, 59 miles are built from Revelstoke and 63 miles from Golden, but thereafter work lags on the province's western half. Parks Canada eventually takes over.

1935 The CPR obtains passenger running rights on the CNR line from Kamloops to Kelowna. The GNR abandons its line in the Fraser Valley, and its line west of Keremeos.

1936 A contract is let for a highway from Radium to Golden. The SS *Sicamous* is retired from service on Okanagan Lake. An era is over.

1937 Relief camps are shut down. Very little is achieved on the Hope–Princeton highway link. The east half of the Big Bend Highway is completed.

1939–40 The province is reported to have 1,150 miles of paved roads, but none of the pavement in the Interior is believed to be of high standard. The Big Bend Highway is opened and the southern route is no longer the only route across the province.

1947 The SS *Nasookin* is retired.

1949 The Hope–Princeton Highway is opened.

1957 The SS *Moyie* is retired from service on Kootenay Lake.

1973 The last CNR rail barge tug goes out of service on Okanagan Lake.

ROAD BULLETIN OF THE AUTOMOBILE CLUB OF SOUTHERN CALIFORNIA, JUNE 1, 1927

Pacific Northwest Washington State

Seattle to Vancouver, B.C., 161 miles.

Continuous pavement is traversed from Seattle by way of Bothel, Silver Lake, Everett, Marysville, Stanwood, Mount Vernon and the Chuckanut Drive (2 miles of which is gravel), Bellingham and Blaine, to Vancouver. A temporary permit, for which no charge is made, is granted for thirty days to motorists visiting Canada. Extensions not to exceed ninety days may be obtained in thirty day periods from any Collector, Customs Officer, or recognized Canadian motor club. The service is free of charge and granted upon request. The Customs Offices at the border are open from 7.00 a.m. to 1.00 a.m. Speed limits in British Columbia are thirty miles per hour on the highway, twenty miles in cities and towns, and ten miles in school areas on regular school days, from 8.00 a.m. to 5 p.m.

Pacific Northwest British Columbia and Alberta

Vancouver to Cache Creek, 286 miles.

Leaving Vancouver via Main Street and Kingsway pavement prevails over the Pacific Highway to Frye's Corner from where good gravel is used to Hope, except for two miles of pavement at Langley, and eight miles of pavement at Chilliwack. At Hope one may ship by train to Princeton, charge 77 c. per 100 pounds, with minimum 5000 pounds. Or drive north over good gravel and natural gravel road through the scenic Fraser Canyon via Lytton and Lillooet to Cache Creek.

Cache Creek to Osoyoos via Kamloops and Enderby, 296 miles, via Princeton 216 miles.

Via Kamloops a fair to poor dirt road, winding and hilly extends through the sage brush country to Savona, with good gravel road to the limits of Kamloops, and pavement into town. Gravel road is then used for 7 miles with fair dirt, poor when wet, to within 9 miles of Salmon Arm, followed by good gravel road via Vernon to Kelowna. It is here necessary to ferry across Okanagan Lake (charges $1.00 per car and 10 cents per passenger). A good type graveled road is then resumed via Penticton to Osoyoos. Via Princeton good natural gravel road, poor when wet, parallels the Thompson River to Spences Bridge with good gravel and short stretches of dirt via Merritt to Princeton, thence down the Similkameen Valley to Keremeos and Osoyoos.

Osoyoos to Cranbrook, 275 miles.

Turning easterly a fair sandy road climbs over Anarchist Mountain, (elevation 3800 ft.), thence fair to good natural gravel down through Kettle Valley to Midway. The same type of road winds through easy grades through a mountainous country to Grand Forks and Cascade from where good two-lane natural gravel road is used to Rossland and Trail, thence along the Kootenay River to Castlegar [*A mistake—it is the Columbia River*] where a free government ferry is used to cross the Columbia River. The same type of good natural gravel is then used to Nelson where it is necessary to ferry Kootenay Lake to Kuskanook Landing. The ferry leaves Nelson daily at 6.30 a.m., and leaves Kuskanook daily at 4.10 p.m. The charges are from $5.00 to $7.00 according to the size of the car, and $2.20 per passenger. From Kuskanook Landing a fair natural gravel road is traversed via Creston to Yahk wth good gravel to Cranbrook.

Cranbrook to Banff and Lake Louise, 186.5 miles.

For details on this route see "Spokane to Lake Louise and Banff."

Spokane to Lake Louise and Banff, 379 miles.

Pavement extends easterly to the Idaho State Line, followed by gravel surfaced highway via Rathdrum and Sandpoint to a point five miles beyond Bonners Ferry. The next 5 miles is fair dirt, then good dirt via Addie to Eastport and Kingsgate. Fair dirt road then extends to Yahk, with good gravel to Cranbrook and Windermere, except for two miles of dirt at Canal Flats. A very good gravel highway is then traversed via Sinclair Canyon and over Vermilion Pass (elevation 5264 feet), and thence to Lake Louise and Banff.

Notes

Chapter 1: The Road Down the Valley

1. G.P.V. and Helen Akrigg, *British Columbia Chronicle 1847–1871*, pp. 123-27.
2. Newton H. Chittenden, *Travels in British Columbia*, pp. 54–61. There is more on Chittenden's travels in chapter 5, The Other B.C. Ferries.
3. For much of the information on early settlers and remittance men and women in the Okanagan and Kootenay valleys I am indebted to recollections provided by longtime residents of the two valleys interviewed for *Bright Sunshine and a Brand New Country*, compiled and edited for the Provincial Archives' Aural History Program by David Mitchell and Denis Duffy.
4. Patrick A. Dunae, *Gentleman Emigrants*, pp. 49, 60, 123–45, 206. Primogeniture was abolished in England in 1925.
5. Frank A. Clapp, *Ministry of Transportation and Highways, Lake and River Ferries*, pp. 54, 55, 77. Peter Lequime was an early rancher who came in 1862. Lloyd Jones came later.
6. Department of Public Works files 212 and 1643. These files also contained the 1902 and 1914 road reports mentioned earlier.
7. Turner, *Sternwheelers and Steam Tugs*, pp. 191-93.

Chapter 2: The Road Up the Lake

1. The Erickson and Lister benches, lying on the east side of the river and south of Creston, provide about 20,000 acres of arable land, the north half of which is largely occupied by orchards, while the south half is devoted to general agriculture and the growing of alfalfa. The Creston Flats, fully reclaimed, were said to be 32,000 acres. They include Duck Lake, a wildlife reserve thanks to Wes Black.
2. Fred J. Smyth, *Tales of the Kootenays*, pp. 8–17, 22–31.
3. G.P.V. and Helen Akrigg, *1001 British Columbia Place Names*, pp. 14, 161–62.
4. Smyth, *Tales of the Kootenays*, p. 23.
5. There was a road through the Fraser Canyon between 1865 and 1894, but it was destroyed when the CPR went through. In 1909, Richard McBride approved construction of a second rail line, the Canadian Northern Pacific (which became the CN), through the canyon, which dashed all hopes of a road connection on that route prior to the First World War.
6. Department of Public Works file 5784-1.

7. For the full text of the Automobile Cub of Southern California road bulletin, dated June 1, 1927, see Appendix 3.

8. The shallow depth of sternwheelers' hulls reduced their strength, especially when they were made of wood. Some had to have steel cable stays added above deck to compensate for this, but this was not practical for the *Nasookin*.

9. Patrick Philip was both deputy minister and public works engineer from 1922 to 1930. His title was then changed to Deputy Minister and Chief Engineer, and finally simply Chief Engineer. He was one of the founders of the Association of Professional Engineers of British Columbia and one of its first presidents at the start of the 1920s.

10. Smyth, *Tales of the Kootenays*, p. 43.

Chapter 3: The Crows Nest Railway

This chapter was based on an article previously published in the *British Columbia Historical News* 37, no. 3 (Summer 2004). The author received the 2004 British Columbia Historical News "Best Article" Award for the article.

1. Anyone could petition a provincial legislature or the federal parliament for a railway charter, but realistically, for a provincial railway an individual had to have the support of an MLA, and for an interprovincial railway he needed an MP and finally a senator onside. A person with public support and funding could proceed initially without political allies, but he would find them necessary when it came time to acquire provincial or Dominion lands, extract government assistance and expropriate private land. It was always a political bargaining process.

2. Creston old-timer Edward Haskins rode this line. He said there were "three trains a week, not enough to keep the weeds down. On a stiff grade the train was stopped by the grease on the weeds. Passengers picked flowers while the crew cut weeds." This is evidence that the area had a very wet cycle of climate in the 1880s. Haskins had helped build the line for $1.50 for each long day of railroading. (From Will Stuart, *Some We Have Met and Stories They Have Told.*)

3. The Crows Nest Pass Agreement was suspended from 1919 to 1922 and disposed of completely in the 1980s because of losses by the CPR and complaints from beef shippers in the Prairies who did not receive the subsidized rate.

4. A man named William Stuart Cameron interviewed many old-timers in the Creston area, and he recorded their stories in a booklet entitled *Some We Have Met and Stories They Have Told*. He used the pen name Will Stuart, and Creston Review Ltd. published it as a centennial project. An extraordinary number of these Creston retirees were veterans of the

railway, and the names of a few appear in this text—Clem Payette, Ernest Hoskins, Henry Raglin, James Compton. Will Stuart's accounts have been of the greatest value to this writing.

Chapter 4: Weather and Roads in British Columbia

1. The highways department built up very good relations with the Japanese highways authority in the late 1970s. This included a visit to Japan by an engineer of the department (P.J. Carr, P.Eng.) for several months to advise them on snow removal methods. This paid off. The chief engineer of the Japanese Toll Highway Authority made a special trip from Tokyo to Vancouver simply and solely to take the B.C. deputy minister of Highways to dinner to thank him for sending the engineer. He had two Japanese civil engineering students from Washington State University come to the meeting as interpreters. He was a charming man, displaying model Japanese politeness!

2. Richard J. Cannings and Sydney G. Cannings, *British Columbia: A Natural History*, p. 41.

3. The overall remedial work at Stewart was under the supervision of R.E. McKeown, Prince Rupert district superintendent, Department of Highways. Contractors working on the Stewart-Cassiar Highway helped him by making resources available, and the highways construction supervisors also helped substantially.

4. At Quesnel, the local organization and management of ice removal and bridge and other repairs was under the supervision of A.L. Slater (P.Eng.), Quesnel district engineer, Department of Highways, and the operation was carried out by Jim Titus and other foremen, by J.M. Hamilton (P.Eng.), Prince George regional maintenance engineer, Department of Highways, and by powderman Ed Miller.

5. The helicopter was supplied by Okanagan Helicopters. Egan Agar was the pilot.

6. The engineer who accompanied all helicopter trips was P.J. Carr (P.Eng.) Prince George regional maintenance engineer, Department of Highways.

7. At both Smithers and Quesnel, overall "on site" control was by R.G. Harvey (P.Eng.), Prince George regional highway engineer, Department of Highways.

8. The powderman at Smithers was Vern Kingsley from the Department of Highways, Kamloops, who was flown in by the personal order of the minister of Highways.

9. Local organization and support for the ice removal and bridge replacement at Smithers was by S.J. Sviatko, Smithers district superintendent, Department of Highways, aided by P. Dunn, Burns Lake district superintendent,

Department of Highways. The bridge replacement work was supervised and carried out by bridge foremen Roy Raby, Dean Barlow, Art Olsen and Angus Kerr, from Smithers, Prince George, Terrace and Burns Lake, respectively, and their crews.

10. The work was supervised by W.R. Kimble, mechanical foreman at Cloverdale, under the direction of E.A. Lund (P.Eng.), director of Equipment Services.

11. This report is based on a news sheet handed out by the ministry at its display at Expo 86. Deas Communications Engineering of Delta, B.C., designed and built the computer controls. The hydraulic drive manifold was designed and developed by Modular Controls of Burlington, Ontario. The proportionate valves were from Lucas Fluid Power of Richmond, B.C., and Western Scales Company of Port Coquitlam, B.C., designed and built the load cells. The front-mounted power roll-over plow (Model R09) was from Frink Canada in Cambridge, Ontario, and Len Barkley International of Victoria supplied the truck. This work was conceived, initiated and supervised by the Equipment Services Branch, and the work was carried out in both the Langford and Cloverdale fabrication shops, with the involvement of the manufacturers.

Chapter 5: The Other B.C. Ferries

The writer is indebted to Frank A. Clapp for his assistance, which was so readily given to this writing, and to the late R.J. Baines and Frank for their dedication throughout the years as unofficial highways historians.

1. This information came from a letter from D.L. Swan to the writer, dated August 27, 1995. The bridge contract was called in 1924, along with one to build a new road on top of the trail from Yale to Spuzzum. The bridge, a 277-foot suspension span with a 90-foot steel truss approach span, was finished in 1926. Unrealistically estimated at $45,000 (the cost of the original bridge in 1863), it ended up costing $92,000. An excellent bridge, it withstood 10 years of very heavy winters following its opening and came well through the 1948 flood. It stayed in service until 1962 and benefited greatly from an open grid steel deck installed later in its life.

Dennis Swan remembers most clearly the very large gravel trucks and the hugely noisy gravel crusher in the Saddle Rock gravel pit that produced crushed gravel pieces as big as eggs. In order to test the strength of the bridge when it was finished, six of the gravel trucks, fully loaded, were placed on the bridge along with three cars (including the Swans'), the only other vehicles available. They were all started up, and together they accelerated at full throttle. This was the ultimate test, and fortunately for the drivers, the bridge sustained it perfectly.

Dennis Swan also remembers the silk trains roaring through Spuzzum, usually late at night. His father went on to become the assistant district engineer at Port Alberni and then the district engineer at Victoria.

2. Mrs. Smith's memoir was titled *Widow Smith of Spence's Bridge* and was edited by J.M. Campbell and A. Ward, pp. 26, 27, 39–41.

3. Information for these items comes from the Department of Public Works Annual Reports, Frank Clapp's writings and the author's personal experience.

4. Kootenay Bay was not included as a stop for the *Nasookin*. When the substitute ferry service went into effect, using the SS *Moyie* and a rail transit barge, a temporary ramped landing had to be built alongside the landing installed for the MV *Anscomb*.

5. R.G. Harvey, *The Coast Connection*, p. 130.

6. Earle Westwood was a Social Credit cabinet minister representing Nanaimo and the Islands. He served consecutively between 1952 and 1963 as minister of Trade and Industry, then Recreation and Conservation and finally Commercial Transport.

7. Ministry of Highways and Public Works, Annual Report 1977–78, pp. 161, 162.

8. "Heavy Waves Greet New Ferry Service," Victoria *Times*, November 10, 1955, p. 1.

9. BC Ferries' small island routes on the coast are: Cormorant, Cortes, Denman, Gabriola, Hornby, Malcolm, Moresby and Quadra. The remote centre is Woodfibre. The rest are subsidized private routes.

10. Ministry of Transportation, Communications and Highways, Annual Report 1979–80, pp. 310, 311.

Chapter 6: The Trek of the Huscrofts in 1891

Most of The Trek of the Huscrofts was first published in somewhat similar form in the *British Columbia Historical News*, vol. 35, no. 2, Spring 2002.

1. In 1883 J.C. (Charlie) Rykerts established a customs post on the east bank of the river at the point the Kootenay re-entered the province. He was later joined by his wife, Ella. The place was named after him, but it attracted no settlers until the Huscrofts arrived.

2. An excellent account of the Church of Latter-day Saints is contained in the *Encyclopaedia Britannica*. The Mormons accepted recruits from all races, including African-Americans and Natives, which was one reason for the opposition to them in the United States.

3. Factual data for this came from Brian Tierney et al., eds., *The Industrial Revolution—Blessing or Curse to the Working Man?* and also contains

input from Arthur Herman's *To Rule the Waves*, p. 447. Child labour is an awful condemnation of that society. The Combination Act was repealed in 1824.

4. William Wise wrote, in his book on the Mountain Meadows Massacre: "and then the expulsion from Nauvoo, the Hain's Hill Massacre, and the murder of Joseph and Hyram Smith in a Carthage gaol would finally be avenged, and John Doyle Lee, as agent of that vengeance, would know the joy of bringing down the Bloody Wrath of God on the hated Gentiles." This was quoted in Appendix I of Sommerfeld and Young's *Family History*, page 3. The *Family History* also gives *Encyclopedia Britannica*, 11th edition, and William A. Linn's *The Story of the Mormons* (1902; repr. New York: Russell and Russell, 1963) as references.

5. The information on the family's life in Utah and their movement east and west again comes from Sommerfeld and Young's *Family History*.

6. Further information on the Mormons in Utah comes from John D. Unruh, *The Plains Across*, pp. 302–307, and from Wilda Sandy, *Jim Bridger*, quoted in Unruh's book.

7. This information is from a paper submitted in a university history course by Dawn Elaine Sommerfeld (née Huscroft) and reprinted in Sommerfeld and Young's *Family History*.

8. The idea of diverting the headwaters of the Kootenay originated with David McLoughlin, the son of Dr. John McLoughlin, the pioneer of the HBC in Oregon, and it was the subject of a letter in the *Spokane Falls Chronicle* of September 1881. (This information was provided by R.J. Welwood in a letter to the *British Columbia Historical News*, Summer 2002 issue.)

9. Baillie-Grohman purchased the *Midge* from a friend in England after canvassing boat-builders in the west and finding them too expensive. The *Midge* was a pleasure boat from Norway made of teak. It was originally the *Midget*, according to some reports, and this was a more suitable name as it was the smallest steamboat on record. The "t" got dropped somewhere between England and Canada. En route from Europe it ran into customs trouble in Montreal due to a crackdown on out-of-Canada steamships. A friendly customs officer agreed to classify it as "agricultural machinery" because Baillie-Grohman said he would use it to cultivate land—land under water! It took three weeks of hard labour to haul it on rollers the 40 miles from Sandpoint to Bonners Ferry, and the owner described the cost of transport as "unconscionable." (Thanks are due to the *Creston Valley Advance* for this information).

10. It is reported that Baillie-Grohman first saw the Kootenay Flats from the top of Arrow Mountain while hunting with Theodore Roosevelt. In 1883 he signed a 10-year lease with the B.C. government for 47,000 acres to be

reclaimed on the flats. He did not personally retain one acre, leaving the area for the last time in 1891.

11. Apart from those kept for farming, the balance of these 50 horses was later sold to mining companies in the Slocan District.

12. They had nothing to fear from the Flatheads or their cousins, the Pend d'Oreille, because, according to *A Guide to the Northern Pacific Railway* put out in 1883, these Natives boasted that they had never killed a White man. The Flathead Indian Reservation was run by Jesuit fathers and had many members of mixed races claiming ancestry from Hudson's Bay Company servants or French Canadians.

13. The Kootenay River and Kootenay Lake were originally named Flatbow River and Flatbow Lake. The river was also christened McGillivray's River by the fur traders, and for a while it was "Flatbow or McGillivray River". The earlier naming, according to the new authority on mapping, Derek Hayes' *Historical Atlas of British Columbia and the Pacific Northwest,* went out of usage soon after 1845, but appeared on many maps to the end of the century, by which time everyone knew them as Kootenay river and lake. The Trutch map of 1871 shows them as that.

14. In 1882 it was reported that there were only 11 White residents in the entire East Kootenay area.

15. J.C. Rykerts' wife, Ella, was the daughter of Henry Wells, a pioneer of American transportation. He was one of the organizers of the Wells Fargo Company, which served the California gold rush and ran stagecoach lines from Sacramento to Salt Lake City and to Portland, Oregon. Theodore Roosevelt stayed with the Rykertses for a few days during his visit to B.C. with William Baillie-Grohman.

16. Creston was built on land formerly owned by a man called Fred Little, who would not sell unless the railway named it after his home town in the United States.

17. The conflict between these railway leaders is described in chapter 3 of this book. Information on the SS *Nelson* is contained in Robert D. Turner's *Sternwheelers and Steam Tugs*. More on the mining boom in the Kootenays is in Fred J. Smyth's *Tales of the Kootenays*.

18. The Huscroft family history records that in the high-water period of 1894 there were several violent wind and rain storms. One of these coincided with their move from the flats to the bench, and it almost achieved what the flooding first threatened—the loss of their possessions. Another such storm later on was less forgiving to the *Midge*; it sank. Just how this happened is unknown, but it was refloated.

19. Mount Huscroft is a peak in the Purcells close to the Kootenay River. It is named in honour of Dennis Huscroft, who was killed by artillery fire in

Germany a few days before the war ended in 1945. Huscroft, a grandson of George Huscroft, was a lieutenant in the Canadian Scottish Regiment. In an article entitled "Just Another Night Patrol" in the February 10, 1945, issue of the *Star Weekly*, CBC war correspondent Matthew Halton wrote about his bravery in leading two patrols behind enemy lines in one night and successfully taking a prisoner for interrogation. Dennis had gotten married during the war, and his first (and only) child was born shortly before these events. Dennis never saw his son.

20. Information for this came from B.R. Atkins' *Columbia River Chronicles* and from Norm Hacking's "Steamboat Days on the Upper Columbia and the Upper Kootenay."

21. Following this reunion, at which a draft of the publication was reviewed, a 494-page volume, *William Rodger Huscroft, Jane (Fisher) Huscroft Family History*, was produced by Dawn (Huscroft) Sommerfeld and John A.I. Young, (Emma's grandson). It was organized by Roots III genealogy software and desktop-published by John Young.

Appendix I: Turning an Engineer into an Author

This writing largely follows an address given by the author to the Fellows of the Canadian Society for Civil Engineering in Victoria, B.C., on May 30, 2001, prior to the 29th Annual Conference of the Society. The text of the address was subsequently used for a Working Paper (number 9/2001) of the same title, which was issued by the EIC History and Archives Committee of the Engineering Institute of Canada and its member societies in December 2001. At this meeting the author received the W. Gordon Plewes Award, "in recognition of his many contributions to the preservation of the history of transportation in B.C."

1. Helen Akrigg's father was Ernest C. Manning, for whom Manning Park was named. He was chief forester of the province for many years, and he was a steadfast conservationist and environmentalist.

2. R.C. Harris, "The First Alexandra Bridge, Fraser Canyon, 1863 to 1912," *B.C. Historical News*, Fall 1982, pp. 8–14, available from the B.C. Archives and Record Service. The "Report by Sapper James Turnbull, R.E., of an Exploration of the Coquihalla River Valley in 1862" is available in the annotated "Edgar Dewdney Papers" held by the Glenbow Archives in Calgary, Alberta.

3. Fraser abhorred the diminutive "Alex," much preferring to be called "Alec."

BIBLIOGRAPHY

Akrigg, G.P.V. and Helen B. Akrigg. *British Columbia Chronicle 1847–1871: Gold and Colonists.* Vancouver: Discovery Press, 1977.

——. *1001 British Columbia Place Names.* Vancouver: Discovery Press, 1969.

Atkins, B.R. *Columbia River Chronicles.* Vancouver: The Alexander Nicholls Press, 1976.

Baillie-Grohman, W.A. "Pioneering in the Kootenays," from Art Downs, ed., *Pioneer Days in British Columbia, Vol. 1.* Surrey, BC: Heritage House Publishing Company, 1973.

B.C. Department of Public Works. Files 212, 1643 and 5784-1.

B.C. Department of Public Works. Report of the Minister, fiscal years 1924–25 through 1929–30 and 1942–43 through 1950–51.

B.C. Ministry of Highways & Public Works. Annual Report, 1977–78.

B.C. Ministry of Transportation, Communication & Highways. Annual Report, 1979–80.

B.C. Ministry of Transportation & Highways. Annual Reports, fiscal years 1981–82 through 1985–86.

Cannings, Richard J. and Sydney G. Cannings. *British Columbia: A Natural History.* Vancouver: Greystone Books, 1996.

Chittenden, Newton H. *Travels in British Columbia.* 1882. Republished with the permission of W. Chittenden. Vancouver: Gordon Soules Book Publishers, 1984.

Clapp, Frank A. *Department of Highways Ferries.* Victoria: B.C. Department of Highways, 1973.

——. *Ministry of Transportation and Highways Inland and Coastal Ferries.* Victoria: Ministry of Transportation & Highways, 1981.

——. *Ministry of Transportation and Highways, Lake and River Ferries.* Victoria: Ministry of Transportation & Highways, 1991.

Downs, Art. *Paddlewheels on the Frontier, Volume 2.* Surrey, BC: Foremost Publishing, 1971.

Dunae, Patrick A. *Gentlemen Emigrants.* Vancouver: Douglas & McIntyre, 1981.

Fraser, Colin. *The Avalanche Enigma.* London: John Munroe, 1966.

Gold, L.W. and G.B. Williams, eds. *Ice Engineering and Avalanche Forecasting and Control.* Technical Memorandum No. 98. Ottawa: National Research Council of Canada Associate Committee on Geotechnical Research, 1970.

Hacking, Norman R. "Steamboat Days in the Upper Columbia and Upper Kootenay." *B.C. Historical Quarterly* 16, Nos. 1 and 2, January–April, 1952.

Harvey, R.G. *Carving the Western Path: By River, Rail, and Road Through Central and Northern B.C.* Surrey, BC: Heritage House Publishing, 1999.

———. *Carving the Western Path: By River, Rail, and Road Through B.C.'s Southern Mountains.* Surrey, BC: Heritage House Publishing, 1998.

———. *The Coast Connection.* Lantzville, BC: Oolichan Books, 1994.

———. "Removal of Two Spans of the Bulkley River Bridge at Smithers by Ice Jam—April 8, 1966." Letter to Deputy Minister of Highways, Victoria, B.C., dated April 27, 1966, file, Region 4, Skeena East R4-E34-40-0.

———. "Account of Emergency Conditions Experienced in Winter of 1961-62." Report on file in Region #4, Department of Highways, Prince George, B.C.

Hayes, Derek. *Historical Atlas of British Columbia and the Pacific Northwest.* Delta, BC: Cavendish Books, 1999.

Herman, Arthur. *To Rule the Waves.* New York: HarperCollins, 2004.

Lamb, W. Kay. *History of the Canadian Pacific Railway.* New York: Macmillan Publishing, 1977.

Luchetti, Cathy. *Women of the West.* St. George, UT: Antelope Island Press, 1982.

Mitchell, David and Denis Duffy, eds. *Bright Sunshine and a Brand New Country: Recollections of the Okanagan Valley 1890–1914.* Sound Heritage, Vol. 8, no. 3. Victoria: B.C. Ministry of Provincial Secretary & Government Services, Provincial Archives, 1979.

Nelson, J.W. *Problems Caused by Avalanches on Highways in British Columbia.* Victoria: B.C. Department of Highways, 1970.

Peck, J.W. *Mining Versus Avalanches: British Columbia.* Victoria: B.C. Department of Mines and Petroleum Resources, 1970.

Sanford, Barrie. *McCulloch's Wonder.* North Vancouver: Whitecap Books, 1977.

Smith, Jessie Ann. *Widow Smith of Spence's Bridge.* Meryl J. Campbell and Audrey Wood, eds. Merritt, BC: Sonotek Publishing, 1984.

Smyth, Fred J. *Tales of the Kootenays.* Vancouver: Douglas & McIntyre, 1977.

Sommerfeld, Dawn Elaine and John A.I. Young, eds. *William Rodger Huscroft, Jane (Fisher) Huscroft Family History.* Privately published by John A.I. Young, 1993.

Stuart, Will [W.S. Cameron]. *Some We Have Met and Stories They Have Told.* Creston, BC: The Creston Review Ltd., 1958.

Tierney, Brian, et al., eds. *The Industrial Revolution in England: Blessing or Curse to the Working Man?* Random House Industrial Series 16. New York: Random House, 1967.

Turner, Robert D. *Sternwheelers and Steam Tugs.* Victoria: Sono Nis Press, 1984.

Unruh, John D., Jr. *The Plains Across: The Overland Emigrants and the Trans-Mississippi West, 1840–60.* Chicago: University of Illinois Press, 1979.

Wise, William. "Massacre at Mountain Meadows." New York: Thomas Y. Crowell, 1976.

Index

Photo Credits

B.C. Archives: pp. 17 (top, H-01001), 20 (F-04995), 81 (D-07653), 153 (I-21301)

B.C. Ministry of Transportation: pp. 17 (bottom), 18, 34 (top), 46 (bottom), 49, 50, 103, 124 (bottom),131

B.C. Forest Service: p. 76 (top)

Clapp, Frank A.: pp. 25 (top and bottom), 107, 109 (left and right), 119, 122, 123, 125 (top and bottom), 128, 129 (bottom)

Glenbow Archives: p. 56

Greater Vernon Museum & Archives: p. 19

Harvey, R.G.: pp. 29, 30, 33, 34 (bottom), 38, 46 (top), 71, 72 (right and left) 74 (top, middle and bottom), 76 (bottom), 77 (right, left and bottom), 78 (top and bottom), 87 (top, middle and bottom), 89, 91, 92, 94, 98, 100, 101, 118, 124 (top), 129 (top), 144

Heritage House Collection: pp. 11, 39, 57, 145

Huscroft family: p. 156

Kelowna Centennial Museum: p. 24

Read more about the pioneer road builders, railway barons, sternwheeler captains and political players in B.C.'s unique transportation history in these three other titles by R.G. Harvey:

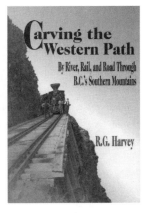

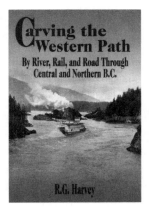

Carving the Western Path

By River, Rail, and Road Through B.C.'s Southern Mountains
" ... contains some brilliant patches ... and some downright howlers. Highly entertaining and informative reading."
—*BC Historical News*
1-895811-62-7 $18.95

By River, Rail, and Road Through Central and Northern B.C.
" ... a good, comprehensive narrative transportation history of northern B.C. from pioneer days to the present."
—*BC Historical Federation*
1-895811-74-0 $16.95

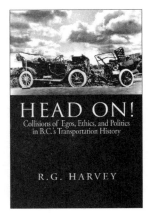

Head On!
Collisions of Egos, Ethics, and Politics in B.C.'s Transportation History
1-894384-75-X $17.95

Visit www.heritagehouse.ca for more great titles from Heritage House.

Bob Harvey was born in Scotland and graduated from the University of Glasgow with a degree in civil engineering in 1943. He immediately joined the British army and served in the U.K., India and Burma before being placed on reserve as a captain (EME) in 1947. He emigrated to Canada in 1948 and joined the B.C. Department of Public Works that same year. In 1950 he married Eva Huscroft, a granddaughter of William Rodger Huscroft. He was the district engineer at Nelson from 1950 to 1954 and the regional highway engineer at  Prince George from 1958 to 1967. He was appointed Deputy Minister of Highways and Public Works in 1976, and he retired from that position in 1983. He has written four books prior to this one, all on the transportation history of British Columbia.